MASSACHUSETTS

\#PELHAM
X AMHERST

CONNECTICUT RIVER

X SPRINGFIELD

X BOSTON

HOUSATONIC RIVER

WINDHAM
X

NEW LONDON

THAMES

X GROTON
X

RHODE ISLAND

DANBURY X
X
HUMPHREYSVILLE

X
REDDING

NEW
HAVEN
X

X STRATFORD
X
COMPO

ROUTE

LONG ISLAND

BROTHER SAM AND ALL THAT:

HISTORICAL CONTEXT AND LITERARY

ANALYSIS OF THE NOVELS OF

JAMES AND CHRISTOPHER COLLIER

by

Christopher Collier

with an essay by

James Lincoln Collier

The Clearwater Press
Orange, Connecticut

BROTHER SAM AND ALL THAT

ISBN 0-9667657-0-2

DEDICATION:

To the many, many teachers
and librarians whose enthusiasm
for our books inspired this one.

INTRODUCTION

I have written this collection of essays for teachers who use our historical novels in their classrooms. I aim to assist especially those who teach American History. The genesis of the eight novels I have written with my brother lies in my own experience teaching eighth graders.

As a beginning teacher in the mid-1950s I soon became disillusioned with the textbook-discussion-test school of pedagogy. Students who earned 100's on their quizzes had forgotten it all two days later. Teaching kids things they would remember for only a day or two was not the way I wanted to spend the rest of my life. Well over forty years later, I am still working on techniques to make learning more complete and more long-lasting. One of those techniques involves the use of novels in the classroom, the subject of the first essay in this collection.

In the 1950s, junior high schoolers were still reading novels for fun—at least girls were; boys less so. It was not unusual for twelve- and thirteen-year-olds to read for recreation and relaxation novels as long as *Gone With the Wind*, as "adult" as *Of Mice and Men*, or as challenging as *The House of the Seven Gables*. It occurred to me that retrospective historical novels written with an avowed intent to teach, with sound historical craftsmanship and historiographic sophistication might bring real historical understanding to teenaged kids.

I had not written a novel, had no practical knowledge of how to go about the job. My brother had, however, and a collaboration looked like the way to go. How we go about these joint efforts is the subject of my brother's essay below.

My academic specialty is early American history, the era from about 1750 to 1801. That was a logical point for us to begin. But more specifically, I wanted to write an antidote to *Johnny Tremain*, used widely to teach about the American Revolution. My analysis of why that novel—despite all its fine literary values—is not appropriate for inculcating a sound understanding of the Revolution constitutes the third essay in this collection.

The eight essays that constitute the core of this book comprise a series of analyses of each of our novels. Each essay includes a discussion of the historical context of the work, a literary and historical analysis, a discussion of the real and fictional characters, and other miscellaneous information, including illustrations and maps, which I think will help teachers help their students to draw out of the novels the historical information and ideas that are there. Each essay can be read by itself without reference to the others. I've made your work easy; you don't have to read the whole book. I hope it works for you. It's been fun for me.

The final essay in this collection recounts my adventures as—with my brother—a pair of America's most censored authors.

CONTENTS

— MAPS —

ILLUSTRATIONS

I. Historical Novels in the Classroom: What They Can Do and How They Should Do It

(Reprinted with permission from the *Bulletin* of the
Children's Literature Assembly, Spring 1982)

The point in studying history is to make oneself more effective and diminish the chances of surprise in meeting new situations. One is more likely to achieve both individual goals—such as getting to a meeting at the right place and the right time—and social goals—such as persuading a school board not to remove *Soul On Ice* from library shelves—if strategic decisions and plans of action are based on an accurate knowledge of what has happened in similar situations in the past. Thus the study of history is important to individuals because it provides them with a memory of not only their own experience—the memory you used to find your way to this room at this time—but also with the memory of any society at any past time—the historical memory. Such an indispensable memory comes to us vicariously—through books, for the most part.

Historians study primary sources from which they attempt to construct the past which they interpret to other historians and—to a certain extent—to the general public through their secondary accounts. By and large these secondary accounts are not written so as to appeal to the general reading public. Most of the people who read books written by historians are coerced into it by school and college teachers. Most Americans learn most of their "history" from novels, films and television. What they learn and what they base important policy decisions on is usually—and I write the word "usually" only after due consideration—not an accurate portrayal of the past, and as a matter of fact frequently is historical nonsense.

Take the case of *Gone With the Wind*, a novel read by millions, and seen on the movie or television screen by countless millions more. When it is time to make policy decisions by casting votes, serving on committees, or merely taking a stance in local and institutional situations about, let us say affirmative action programs, vast millions of Americans believe that the slave experience was benign and that American blacks have had all the help they need or deserve. The source of popular wisdom about slavery is drawn from a work whose "history" is pure fiction. Such works can be positively damaging to society because they mislead the public about conditions that prevailed in the past. (Not nearly so damaging, however, as any effort to suppress them.)

My first point, then, is that it is vitally important in a society in which most people may vote and in which many people are socially influential that an accurate understanding of the relevant past be widespread. My second point is that most people derive their impression of the past from popular history. The conclusion, inevitably, is that popular history, if it is to help individuals and society work better, must be as accurate as possible.

I turn now to the subject of historical fiction. I deal with the historical part of that coupling, and the books I write with my brother are written with a pedagogical purpose—to teach about ideals and values that have been important in shaping the course of American history. The first stage of writing each book is the articulation of some concept that I think is important to know and that young teenagers can learn. *The Bloody Country*, for instance, is about the relative balance of human values and property values; *The Winter Hero* depicts the economic basis of politics; *Jump Ship To Freedom* describes the relationship of slavery to the framing of the U.S. Constitution of 1787. *My Brother Sam Is Dead* depicts the American Revolution as a civil war and attempts to personify the varieties of attitudes toward and results of the war.

The goal of these books is to:
   1. provide students with information about the past

2. in order to present real historical problems
3. so that students can practice thinking about individual and social problems that have a historical basis
4. which information and practice will provide them with insight and skill in dealing with their own individual and social problems
5. and present all this material in a way that will command their attention and impress their memory.

I have been highly critical of much historical fiction. On what basis do I level such criticism? In the first place I approach the genre from the position of both a historian and a teacher. My criteria reflect that position. I am judging works of historical fiction by their social and pedagogical usefulness—that is, their ability to teach history. Given those assumptions, my criteria are five. The books must:

1. focus on an important historical theme, an understanding of which helps us to deal with the present
2. center on an episode in which the theme adheres to fact
3. attend to the historiographic elements
4. include fictional characters that interact meaningfully (in terms of theme) and interestingly with historical characters
5. present detail accurately.

As briefly as I can, let me explain each of these criteria. The first, given my assumptions and purposes, is self-evident. The second is what distinguishes good and useful historical fiction from the mere costume novel, the overwhelmingly predominant type within the genre. Costume novels are not about the past. They are rather stories that could take place at any era, but which are set in the past. Novelists have their literary reasons for doing this, some of them quite valid from a literary point of view. But such works are rarely good history and inevitably distort the public understanding of the forces that have shaped the present. A useful historical novel will tell a story accurately, the very telling of which brings out and makes clear its central theme. The theme must not be imposed upon the events, and the events themselves must naturally cohere to form the theme. *The Winter Hero*, for instance, was to have been a book about one of the nation's central problems—the tension between liberty and equality; but as I got deep into the research I saw that that theme was not there. It was not necessary to throw away the research, however, because the episodes I found clearly did illuminate another important element of American history—that political differences are often reflections of economic differences.

My third criterion relates to historiography, that is, the way that professional historians have approached and interpreted the central episode of the story. Was the American Revolution an economic conflict? An ideological or constitutional struggle? An outgrowth of imperial policy? A result of local political differences in each colony? One could go on. I develop a thorough understanding of the historical elements and, while making my own judgement about which should predominate, try to see that each of the significant interpretations finds some place in the story.

Historical figures inevitably play a part in a historical novel based on the criteria listed here. The character of the figures should be as they are portrayed by the most-respected biographers, and they should be shown doing things that in fact they did do. Though it is not always essential, even our fictional characters do things that were actually done—sometimes by known, sometimes by anonymous figures from the past.

Finally, the detail should be accurate. This is the easiest, though the most time consuming, of the research that goes into these books. Though it takes years of study to be able to fully understand and appraise the *historiography* of an event, any college history major could learn how to go about finding the detail of material culture in six months or so, and a good reference librarian could master the techniques in a few weeks. But accuracy of detail is important. Nothing so turns off a reader as to find people striking matches in 17th-century Massachusetts, or checking their wrist watches in the middle of the French and Indian War. But there is more to the matter of detail. If you don't get the detail right—how people ate and traveled and what they did each hour to earn a living; how they dressed against a blizzard or what it took to load and fire a musket; how thick the forest, or how wide the river, how high the mountain or rough the storm through which they passed—then you won't have the story right; and there you go perpetuating another myth that will confuse our public policy.

Christopher Collier

Obviously no one is equipped to appraise all the historical novels potentially useful in classrooms on the basis of these criteria. But there are lots of professional historians who are able to make judgements about those in their special fields. If writers consulted appropriate historians; if editors submitted manuscripts to historians for appraisal; and if scholarly journals sent historical novels to historians for review—then the problems visited on society for generation after generation because of the misuse of history might well be alleviated. Without such professional review writers and publishers, teachers and librarians will go on producing and assigning bad historical work.

If, on the other hand, the theme is important; if the episode illustrates the theme; if the interpretation is historiographically sophisticated; if the characters and detail are accurately portrayed—if all that, then of course, readers of the book will learn to make well-informed and knowledgeable decisions about individual and public matters and we will all live happily ever after. Perhaps such works of historical fiction are not quite impossible to write.

II. DOING THE LITERARY TANGO:
Ideas, Words, and Collaboration

James Lincoln Collier
(Reprinted with permission from *The Alan Review*. Winter 1978)

One of the questions I am asked most about my work is how do my brother and I possibly manage to make a joint venture out of an activity as obviously private and personal as writing a book. The reader's puzzlement is understandable: Writing *is* personal, and private. A writer works from a point of view that is his own. He is always saying this is how *I* feel about these things; this is the way it seems to *me*. Indeed, a great deal of what we get from the best writing is a personal view of the world: the irony of Charles Dickens, Hemingway's sense of the world as an adversary, the rueful sentimentality of Laurence Sterne. How, thus, can two people, however close in point of view, bring a single stamp to one work?

In fact, Kit, as Christopher is known to family and friends, and I, as brothers are likely to, do share to a considerable extent a common world view. Our parents had roots deep in New England; but they had left their home culture to move into a somewhat artistic, semi-Bohemian culture in New York. We grew up in this mix of cultures, one side of which valued hard work, human decency, and a respect for the privacy of others; the other of which valued high-minded intellectuality, adherence to principle, and a concern for the truth. (These virtues of course, when pushed too far, can turn into uncharitable inflexibility and self-righteousness.) As far as our writing is concerned, we thus share a view that what we put onto a page ought to be as truthful as we can make it—carefully researched, clearly thought-out and accurately described.

But our approach to writing differs in other ways. Kit sees himself essentially as a teacher, with all that implies. He began his professional career as a seventh-grade social studies teacher, and although he moved into college teaching after a few years because he was drawn to scholarship, he has been a teacher all his life. In the books we do together his goal is to awaken students' curiosity—that is, get them to start asking questions. Readers who know our books will have some idea of what those questions are: Was the Revolution necessary? Who in fact were the patriots in that fight? What is economic freedom, and what is worth sacrificing for it? How did the racism that has been so much a part of the American experience become institutionalized? What has it cost us? I think any teacher who is using our books can mine them for questions like these, and undoubtedly find some of which we are unaware.

My approach to writing is different from Kit's. To me a piece of fiction works in some ways like music—a song, a symphony, an improved jazz chorus. It is something which works on the emotions, and when I write I try deliberately to catch readers up in my story, to make them *feel* things, and in the end, if I am very lucky, to change their internal landscape a little by showing them a new way of looking at the world. My brother and I, although we are both addicted to the truth, otherwise have different aims in creating our books. How do we manage this?

To begin with, we have agreed that at some point in the process the entire story must pass uninterrupted through one consciousness. This is so that there is a consistency of language, of feeling of "tone," a hard-to-define quality that is nonetheless present in most good writing, as for example the aforesaid irony of Dickens and the ruefulness of Stern. Eventually, thus, I will sit down and write the book from start to finish.

But the book begins in Kit's head with an idea or concept he wants to teach, a question he wants to raise in the minds of readers. He casts about for an historical event, or sequence of events, which can illustrate his point. Or rather, the mind being what it is, these arise simultaneously: that is, at one moment he sees both the event, and how he can illustrate a certain point. He then brings the idea to me: There was a black named Jack Arabus who sued for his freedom after the Revolution in an important case, which we might use to say something about the economic basis of freedom. He fills me in, and then I make a judgement about the dramatic possibilities in the idea. Some of the questions I must ask are: Is the story compact in time, so that it does not require too many flashbacks in telling? Is there plenty of action? Is there natural conflict between various of the major characters? Would our young protagonist realistically have a role in the events, rather than merely observing them?

I have to be very careful about this, for I know that there can be no doctoring of the events, no shifting them about in time for as much as a minute, no changing the locale for as much as a yard. And I—we—have made mistakes. For one example, the action in *The Bloody Country* was spread out over too long a time, and we struggled mightily to keep the story glued together. For another, any time you are writing about slaves the action is perforce limited, which almost invariably means that a slave story must be built around an escape. However, the first two books in the Arabus family trilogy involved runaways. This was not the commonest black experience, and out of respect to the truth we did not want to show another black younger person in flight in the third book. Yet a protagonist must always have a purpose, and those who have read *Who Is Carrie?* will see how we solved the problem—again, not without struggle.

Actually, all of this comes about a good deal more informally than the foregoing implies. We live some fifty miles apart, and talk to each other frequently on business, social or family matters. We may or may not be looking for an idea for a new book; that of course depends on our other commitments. But as it usually works, if Kit comes up with an idea that we get enthusiastic about, we are likely to find a way to do it. He then works up a detailed outline: here's the basic sequence of events, here are the characters, here's a rough story outline. I look it over, test it for

10

dramatic problems and possibilities. We sit down together and adjust the outline as necessary so that the story will be both gripping and get the pedagogical point across.

Now we see our editors. We tell them what we want to do, and so far they've agreed; although they always have suggestions about one or another aspect of the books.

The next step is for Kit to supply me with a heap of research—books on the period, scholarly articles on the ideologies involved, maps, drawings, whatever he can find. In addition, either separately or together, we visit the ground where the action will take place. We photograph period houses or features of the landscape, check old maps against new to see how roads and steams may have moved and visit historical museums where they exist.

Once I have digested the research, I sit down and write—pass the story through a single consciousness. It is agreed that I can go anywhere I want with the story at this point. Although of course I write out of the historical background, I feel free to invent as I like, knowing that my brother will in time have opportunity to check for historical accuracy. The point is for me not to feel constrained: If I have a scene working the way I want, I want to be able to plunge forward as the drama leads without having to worry about historical detail.

When I have finished a draft, it goes to Kit. His main task is to check the history, for accuracy of detail and thematic consistency, but he will also make suggestions about the story line: This scene seems flat, this seems improbable and so forth. We discuss the whole once more. Concerning questions he has raised about the story line, if I feel confident that I am right, he will accept my view, once he has argued his position. But questions of historical fact and interpretation are his province, I must abide by his judgement. For example, in *My Brother Sam Is Dead* I wanted, near the beginning, to have the two boys who are at the center of the story to have a discussion out of earshot of their parents, and I set them to washing dishes in the kitchen. This, my brother said, would not do; at that time males did not wash dishes. I had the boys instead go out in the barn to tend the animals, where they could talk without being overheard.

Once we have sorted out these problems—and sometimes matching the story we want to tell with historical reality requires a good deal of nimble inventiveness so as to subvert neither—I write a complete new second draft, of course shoring up weak points of which I am aware. (I have a tendency to keep forging ahead in the first draft, leaving weak scenes to be dealt with later.) This second draft then goes back to Kit, who goes over it once again, and after further discussion, we make such changes as are necessary. These ought to be minor; but a couple of times I had to do substantial revision on this second draft.

Then it goes to the editor. She will have comments. In most cases these are minor—we need to know a little bit more about A's background, it isn't quite clear why B did such-and-such; we ought to have a stronger reaction for C at this point. We can, of course, reject these editorial suggestions, and at times we have; but we have a tendency to accept them because she is bringing a fresh eye to the material we have by this point begun to get a little fed up with. (Both of us are occupied with new projects, and it is always a little irritating to have to turn back to an old one.)

Then, finally, it is done. It is clear that one reason why it all works is there's a pretty strict division of labor in the process. We each have our bailiwicks, and so long as we continue to respect each other's area of expertise—which we do—we can avoid arguments. And, in truth, we have rarely ever had a serious argument, although we have come a few times to compromises with which neither of us was very happy.

Perhaps the most interesting of our collaborations, to me at least, was in the writing of our 1985 study of the Constitutional Convention, *Decision in Philadelphia*. Here we were not dealing with fiction; my role was solely to make readable material of which Kit was entirely in control. I confess that at the outset—

we began thinking about the book in 1979—I knew far less about the Constitution than I ought to have. Once again we agreed that for consistency of tone, the whole book would have to pass through one consciousness. We decided then that Kit would act as my teacher, and take me step-by-step through the Constitutional Convention, following an outline he had devised. Chapter by chapter he gave me heaps of assiduously gathered material: biographies, endless abstruse monographs on subjects I didn't know existed, maps, copies of old newspapers, lists of ship tonnages and exports from American ports, and much more of the stuff of which historical research is made. Chapter by chapter I studied this material, digested it and worked it up into some sort of coherent form. When we finally finished we had a seven-hundred-page manuscript that was hopelessly disjointed, confused, and in many cases wildly incorrect. But now I understood the Constitutional Convention, and we could begin. It would be two more complete drafts before we had the book in shape; but we got to where we wanted to go.

Collaboration, I think, is always difficult. I would not attempt it with just any-one. It is impor-tant to work with someone who can work out ground rules and stick to them, someone who thinks the way you do about most things, and above all, someone with whom you can have a meas-ure of mutual respect.

III. JOHNNY AND SAM —
Old and New Approaches to The American Revolution

(Reprinted from *The Horn Book*, April 1976)

For perhaps the tenth time in as many weeks I listened with
embarrassment as my host introduced me—on this occasion to
about a hundred Connecticut reading specialist—as someone
who had at last found something new to say about the American
Revolution. Surely, I thought, there are some people in my audience who will think me pretentious and recognize the preposter-
ousness of the statement. If, among the thousand of teachers and
librarians I have addressed in the year and a half since the publication of *My Brother Sam Is Dead*, there were those who thought
the statement absurd, none have been so rude as to say so. They
have left that unwelcome job to me.

The embarrassment I have felt on these occasions stems from
the fact that what is seen as new in the book my brother and I
wrote has behind it at least two generations of scholarship among
academic historians. The interpretation of the American
Revolution that informs *Brother Sam* was thoroughly developed
and precisely stated during the first quarter of the 20th century.
Though the historiographic approach is not new, its popularization in juvenile literature apparently is. Indeed, it was largely to
fill an historiographic gap that I was moved to ask my brother,
James Lincoln Collier, to collaborate on the work.
Historiography—the methodology of historical research and the
study of varying historical interpretations—is the great mass of
work that lies beneath the tip of the historical iceberg. The
method, buried in scholarly apparatus, is concealed from the lay
public; and the interpretation is normally so well integrated with
description and narration that nonprofessionals are unaware of it.

14

But all written history is interpretation, and novelists present their own historical interpretation whether they are conscious of it or not. Thus, a particular historiographic view is frequently brought unconsciously to readers, who are bound to absorb it equally unconsciously.

To state it simply, the historiography of the American Revolution breaks down into three schools of thought—the Whig, the Imperialist, and the Progressive. The range of interpretation is vast, of course, and includes 18th-century Patriot and Loyalist presentations as well as Marxist, Stalinist, Freudian, and other off-beat modes. But the main body of secondary literature about the Revolution written over the past century and a half falls into one or the other of these three dominant groups, though some historians combine elements of two of them, and no two interpretations are identical.

The Whig interpretation, which takes its name from the Parliamentary faction opposed to George III's colonial policies, dominated the 19th century during the era before the professionalization of the practice of history. Its principal popularizer was George Bancroft (1800-91), and thus it is frequently referred to as the Bancroftian view. Nineteenth-century Whig historians saw the Revolution as a spontaneous and universal uprising of the colonial yeomanry. Americans, they claimed, had taken up the cause of traditional English liberty in a struggle against the regressive policies of a tyrannical king who was supported by a venal ministry that had, in turn, bought off and corrupted the larger part of Commons. The Whig picture was moralistic and pedantic, depicting simple, freedom-loving farmers marching in a crusade to fulfill God's plan for rationally ordered society based on principles of liberty and equality. The Whig effort wanted to teach a national patriotism based upon a respectful adoration of the principles of natural rights and social contract and of the men who died to protect them. A much more sophisticated version of the Whig interpretation—the 20th-century one—shows a great middle-class America fighting to preserve the right to practice self-government under a universally accepted concept of the British Constitution constructed on Lockean social contract. This viewpoint has dominated professional historiography since World War II, but its 19th-century ancestor has never lost its hold over popular and juvenile literature.

The Bancroftian view of the Revolution came under severe attack by the newly risen class of professional historians during the late 19th- and early 20th- centuries. The entrance of the United States upon its own imperialist adventures in the 1890s together with a developing Anglophilia and a host of other changes in the American political and intellectual climate, drew attention to the English side of the conflict. The Imperialist historians sought a much more objective approach to the conflict and looked for research materials in London as well as in the archives of the former colonies. For them, a true view of the war could only be obtained from the center of the empire looking out. They pointed to the fact that there were twenty-four British American colonies, and the reasons for the loyalty of nearly half of them were certainly as worthy of study as the revolt of the others. The Imperialist historians tend to see the American Patriot position as small-minded, shortsighted, and selfish. They served as a much-needed counterbalance to the flamboyant chauvinism of the filiopietistic Christian gentlemen who wrote history in the Victorian era. The Imperialist historians, however, have had no effect on the writing of popular history or children's literature. But what an intriguing idea: to see the American Revolution through the eyes of a white teenager in Nova Scotia or Quebec or of a black boy in Bermuda or Jamaica—to say nothing of the point of view of a ten-year-old cotton mill worker thrown out on the streets of Manchester as a result of the American embargo!

Though the Imperialists sharply undermined the nationalism of the old Whigs, there is nothing about their interpretation that necessarily requires a British or a world view. One could approach the study of the Revolution from English sources and still conclude that the Americans had been right in their sense of repression and in their understanding of the rights of man. The same cannot be said about the Progressive interpretation.

Arising contemporaneously with the Imperial view, but developing out of domestic rather than world events, the Progressive concept of the Anglo-American conflict of 1763-83 was set against a background of internal political strife, economic motivations, and rapid social changes. As young historians looked about them in the 1890s and the years before World War I, they saw an America wracked by a too-rapid industrialization and urbanization with the accompanying agony of class conflict, the corruption of the political system, and the dominance of economics over ideology. And they read the past through spectacles tinted by the social conditioning of the late 19th-and early 20th-century reform movement known as Progressivism.

The Progressive historians elevated economic impetus—both in its individual and in its collective or class manifestations—above ideological or religious motivations. To them reality was found only in concrete economic fact. They also took the social conflict that engulfed their America—geographically based, class motivated, politically inspired but not, however, generational, sexual or racial as it might be seen today—to be the normal state of events. They turned to sources that would reveal this reality as it existed in the English colonies of the late 18th century. The picture they painted enraged, confused, and ultimately confounded both the old Whigs and the young Imperialists.

The Progressive historians—the most sensational and prolific of whom was Charles A. Beard—developed sufficient evidence to indict the Revolutionary leaders for being interested in throwing off the imperial yoke in order to liberate their own economic and political opportunities; or, at least, to serve the economic interests of a large, though minority, commercial class. The question, in the most famous of all our historiographic phrases, was not only one of home rule, but of *who* should rule at home. As a result of the insights thrown out by the Progressives (and of the needs of thousands of eager dissertation writers), the history of America has been studied and displayed in monograph after monograph of minute investigation of countless local political squabbles, economic biographies of influential figures, and interpretations that assume fundamental conflicts in American society.

During the heyday of Progressive historiography—roughly the period marked by the two World Wars inclusively—the old middle-class consensus on 18th-century liberalism was pictured as a myth of the romantic early 19th century. Really, the Anglo-American conflict was seen as but a by-product of the local economic and political ambitions of a dynamic colonial leadership no longer able to tolerate the restraints of a second-class imperial citizenship. The American War for Independence was only part of a civil war that pitted brother against brother as aristocratic and popular interests struggled to control the policy-making machinery of their respective colonies.

Progressive historiography has, then, a hoary if feisty heritage. However, despite its crude popularization—a caricature really—in the form of debunking biographies so prevalent in the 1920s, the Progressive concept never really permeated popular literature. Furthermore, the unifying events of the 1940s and the 1950s—decades so dominated by ideological shadows of hot and cold wars—dealt a severe blow to its chances for general popular acceptance. For the new Whigs of the postwar generation have revived principle as a motivating force, and consensus, on certain attitudes at least if not on a full blown ideology, as informing the reasons for war in 1775.

The reason, I suspect, that *My Brother Sam Is Dead* appears to say something new is that it stands alone among Revolutionary juvenile literature as an effort to present a view of the war that incorporates elements of both the Whig and Progressive interpretations, with a strong emphasis on the latter. Few children's books on the subject make any attempt to deal with issues at all. For the most part they are merely stories laid in the period and given verisimilitude by incorporating authentic detail.

Consider one of the best of these, Elsie Singmaster's *Rifles for*

Washington, written in 1938 when the Great Depression had given the Progressive interpretation its most dramatic claim to the public attention. One reads through this marvelously detailed and carefully researched work without gaining any idea at all of why Americans were fighting the British army in the first place. "'[T]he people want freedom,'" says Peter at one point; and Uncle Proudfoot quotes Thomas Paine, saying "'the voice of weeping nachure cries it is time to part'"; and fragments of the Declaration of Independence are thrown out as background to a martial scene later on. Once the author seems to notice some political division in American society: An anonymous man stands opposite a graveyard and declares angrily, "'I have rope to hang all the members of Congress . . . We have no grounds for war.'" But the approach is shallow and simplistic, and ultimately the politics are wholly irrelevant to the story that Elsie Singmaster tells so dramatically. *Rifles for Washington* is not actually about the American Revolution; it is just a wonderful story set in the time and place.

Johnny Tremain, of course, is the work that must be dealt with. The year before its publication in 1943 Esther Forbes had written *Paul Revere and the World He Lived In*. Though she was not a trained historian, her *Paul Revere* is listed in the prestigious *Harvard Guide to American History*, a selective work that also puts *Johnny Tremain* in a list of historical novels useful for delineating their eras. Forbes, I venture to say, knew what she was talking about.

Diligently as one may search through *Johnny Tremain*, however, one finds no deviation from the standard Whig treatment. Perhaps Johnny's thought a he watches a British officer slap a wounded enlisted man—"We are fighting, partly, for just that. Because a man is a private is not reason he should be treated like cordwood'"—is a conscious effort on the author's part to note the equalitarianism that the Progressives tended to emphasize as opposed to the Whig's libertarianism. Or again, she shows her awareness of the Imperial school when she has an English doctor say, "'You remember that *we* don't like being here in Boston any

19

better than you like having us . . . We're both in a tight spot. But if we keep our tempers and you keep your tempers, why, we can fix up things between us somehow. We're all one people, you know.'"

Esther Forbes does deal with issues; her story is intrinsically about the American Revolution; a different time and place would make it a different story. She tips her hand early while explaining that the new tea tax would actually reduce the price of tea in the colonies. "Weren't the Americans, after all, human beings?" she has a cynical Parliament ask. "Wouldn't they care more for their pocketbooks than their principles?" The rest of her book demonstrates the reverse. Her treatment is pure 19th-century Bancroft. Her spokesman is James Otis—in real life scorned by 1775 by the radical revolutionaries as too conservative and untrustworthy in his divided loyalties. Forbes depicts him as fallen from leadership not because of political events but because of his increasingly frequent periods of insanity—also historically accurate. She brings Otis back to give, in a crowded, smoky, attic meeting place of the Sons of Liberty, a spirited statement of old-fashioned American Lockeanism.

'For what will we fight?'" demands Otis.

"'We will fight for the rights of Americans. England cannot take our money away by taxes,'" is the reply of Sam Adams.

"'No, no. For something more important than the pocketbooks of our American citizens . . . For men and women and children all over the world . . . There shall be no more tyranny. A handful of men cannot seize power over thousands. A man shall choose who it is shall rule over him.'"

Otis then proceeds to demonstrate that John Hancock will give up his property, Joseph Warren sacrifice his family, Paul Revere his business, and John Adams his career—all to make the world safe for democracy. Sam Adams with his talk of taxes is dismissed: "'what it is really about . . . you'll never know,'" say Otis. "'It is all so much simpler than you think,'" the old firebrand announces after downing a second tankard of punch. "'We all give all we have, lives, property, safety, skills . . . we fight, we die, for a simple thing. Only that a man can stand up.'" Esther Forbes leaves no doubt about her meaning, for the final chapter is entitled "A Man Can Stand Up," and at the close of the profoundly touching description of the events after Lexington and Concord and the death of Johnny's closest friend Rab, Johnny thinks again, "True, Rab had died. Hundreds would die, but not the thing they died for.

"'A man can stand up . . .'"

Johnny Tremain, with its message of ideologically motivated war, is so much the product of World War II that one who grew up in the 1940s must honor its clear one-sidedness. Younger historians, products of the 1960s who are currently (1976) busy reviving the Progressive interpretation of a generation ago, would be less tolerant. But without denying its outstanding literary merit Forbes' presentation of the American Revolution does not pass muster as serious professional history. Not so much because it is so sharply biased but because it is simplistic. Life is not like that—and we may be sure it was not like that two hundred years ago. Such an event as a war involving the three major European nations, with implications for the western power structure for centuries to come, is bound to be a complex matter. To present history in simple, one-sided—almost moralistic—terms is to teach nothing worth learning and to falsify the past in a way that provides worse than no help in understanding the present or in meeting the future.

Perhaps *Brother Sam* benefits from the revolution of our own times in that publishers are ready now to present teenagers with some complex issues and some raw reality to chew on. If there is a ring of novelty in our book about the conflict Americans celebrate this year, (1976) the sound is not in the ears of historians, but only in the ears of children. And that is revolution enough.

21

IV. *My Brother Sam Is Dead*

Historical Context

The Setting

I grew up in Wilton, Connecticut, a southerly neighbor of Redding, the locale of *My Brother Sam Is Dead*. Wilton of the 1930s and 1940s was much like Redding of the 1950s and 1960s when I lived there with my children Ned and Sally, to whom the book is dedicated, and their mother. We lived in a house that was standing at the time the events in *My Brother Sam is Dead* took place. Redding in the 1950s was a small exurban town of about 2,500 people scattered randomly and rather thinly over thirty-two square miles. It was woodsy and pastoral but cluttered with commuters to nearby towns and a few hardy daily travelers to New York City sixty miles to the southwest. In the mid-20th century wooded areas dominated the landscape, and, indeed, covered much more of the hilly terrain than they had during the Revolutionary Era. The population of Redding in 1774 was about half that of 1950, but by the 1770s half a century of cutting had virtually denuded the hills and valleys. The Meeker family could see distances from ridge to ridge, and even to Long Island Sound fifteen miles to the south, that haven't been possible at any time in the 20th century.

Redding, like many Connecticut towns, is situated on a series of north-south ridges bordered on the west by Ridgefield, which is on the New York line, and on the south by Fairfield on the Long Island shore. Redding, in Fairfield County, was one of the colony's seventy-three towns governed by annual and special town meetings and ultimately under the authority of the two-house General Assembly, which met twice yearly.

Connecticut's government was established in 1639 under a self-generated document called the Fundamental Orders. The governmental system set up under the Orders was incorporated into and supplemented by a royal charter granted by Charles II in 1662. The colony was uniquely autonomous and recognized virtually no control from England at all. It was a commercial backwater, and benefitted from the benign neglect characteristic of England's imperial policy before the 1760s. The freemen of Connecticut's towns were accustomed to a very high level of self-government and a very low level of exterior control. They paid small colony-wide taxes, a bit more for town services, and a lot more to support the local churches and schools.

The Congregational Church, derived from Calvinist theology and separatist polity, was established—that is, tax supported—in Connecticut. Until the 1720s everyone was required to attend the local "public" church and pay taxes to support it. Some of these autonomous congregations joined together in "consociations" and agreed to accept a certain amount of guidance in matters of theology and church polity; these were referred to as Presbyterian. The Congregational Church in Redding was one such. In the 1720s Anglican congregations began to organize. The colony government could hardly outlaw the king's own church, so ecclesiastical taxes paid by Anglicans could be diverted to pay their own minister. This privilege was ultimately extended to Quakers and Baptists, but the Congregational establishment continued to hold a privileged place until a new constitution was adopted in 1818.

Redding was established as a collection of individually owned farms called a "particular plantation" in 1729 by John Read. In 1732 the local Congregational minister, John Beach, became an Anglican and split the congregation. Most of Beach's followers lived on the eastern side of town, on the Ridge close to the Anglican Church. Perhaps proximity in those days of foot transportation determined choice of church more than theological conviction. Beach commuted each Sunday to preach in neighboring Newtown as well. He didn't miss a Sunday for fifty years, and died with his pastoral boots on in 1782. Anglicans felt a great kinship with English institutions, prayed regularly for the king, and generally seemed to be more accepting of hierarchical organization. Thus their affinity for Loyalism after 1776. In Beach's apostasy lay the roots of Redding's political division in the Revolutionary Era. When push came to shove and men had to stand up and be counted, a large number—perhaps more than half—of the town's voters stood by the king. The whole population was 1,234 in 1774, which would figure to about 225 town-meeting voters.

Connecticut's towns were organized into "train bands," the militia companies in which almost all men between sixteen and fifty—ministers, government officials, Yale students, and professors, and a few other categories excepted—had to serve. In Redding there were so many Loyalists in the east company in the area on Redding Ridge around the Anglican Church that the General Assembly—overwhelmingly Whig by 1775—disbanded it. Soon Patriot militiamen all over the state went from town to town physically disarming men of known or suspected Loyalist leanings. This was especially the case in Fairfield County, where, perhaps because of its proximity to New York, there was a higher concentration of Anglicans and thus Loyalists.

Though it is not technically correct to use the term Loyalist before 1776, convention equates it with Tory. The terms of Tory and Whig originated in the division during England's Glorious Revolution of 1685-89 which deposed the Catholic James II in favor of Mary and William. Tories wished to continue the old Stuart succession; Whigs did not. Since that time the terms had signified the pro and anti-monarchical factions, if I may put a very complicated situation simply. Thus Whigs in America were Patriots; Tories were Loyalists. In England's Parliament Whigs favored a more liberal policy toward the colonies, less restrictive of colonial self-government, especially in the area of taxation. Edmund Burke, to whom Sam refers (p.8) was a leading Whig member of Parliament and the author of several pamphlets justifying a permissive colonial policy. The terms Whig and Tory were used in the American colonies to designate opponents and supporters of royal and parliamentary taxes and restrictions since at least the Stamp Act crisis of the mid-1760s.

Large numbers of people were neither Whig nor Tory and just wished to get on with their lives—like Life Meeker. Many of these people took sides only when events forced them to, and some reverted to neutralism or switched allegiance when events changed. Historians estimate that perhaps 20 percent of Americans were committed Loyalists—at least a hundred thousand of whom fled the revolting colonies during or right after the war. The New England colonies had lower proportions of Loyalists than elsewhere, and Connecticut was no exception. A few towns like Redding in Fairfield County produced significant numbers of them, however.

The presence of the Church of England in Redding explains the unusually large number of Loyalists in the town. Though by no means were all Anglicans Loyalists, the ranks of the king's followers in Connecticut were drawn largely from that denomination, which reflected a cross section of Connecticut society. Since one of our reasons for writing *My Brother Sam Is Dead* was to portray the American Revolution as a civil war, it was important to situate the story in a heavily Tory town.

One of the points that historians have developed is that religious conviction was weakening in the second half of the 18th century and people became even more this-worldy during the Revolutionary Ear. Religious beliefs permeated Timmy's world, but he begins—perhaps unknowingly—to fall away. Note the casual way he uses profanity from time to time even though he knows it is a sin. When his mother tells Timmy not to worry about God's retribution for the sin of working on the sabbath, (illegal in Connecticut, but the law was not enforced during the war), Timmy says, "I didn't tell her that I wasn't worried." (p.128) Timmy's loss of faith has been a major cost of the events he has lived through. He has drifted a long way from the days when he could say—and believe—that God would visit his wrath upon Sam for disobeying his father (p.29).

Conventional religion was not the only institution that took a beating during the war. The very characteristics that make people human also lose their strength. People, as Mother says, begin to behave like animals: They are brutalized. "The brutes," she says of the British troops invading the town, "War turns men into beasts." (p. 140) "War turns men into animals," (p. 174), and finally, humanity leaves her entirely: "Going to get yourself killed, son," she says to Timmy as he goes off in his fruitless, abortive attempt to rescue Sam. She doesn't even look at him. "You're going to get yourself killed. Well, you might as well. Let's have it all done with at once." (pp. 201-02) And she withdraws, not just from the war as she says but from human association as well. She seems to have become a hollow shell—though we learn from the "Epilogue" that she will survive and to some extent, at least, recover.

NOTE: The page numbers given throughout this essay conform to the hardcover and paperback editions except for one paperback printing with the same cover as the hardback. This printing of 1974 was expurgated by the publishers (without the authors' permission), and the pagination differs from that in all other printings. The original language is complete in all other editions and printings.

The Characters

There were Meeker families in Redding during the years of our story but, of course, we made up those who appear in our account. I have not found Timmys, Sams, Eliphalets [E-life-a-let], or Susannahs among them, nor do I find that any of them ran a tavern. But all the things that happen to them in our story did, in fact, happen to someone in real life.

There is no Read named Betsy. The granddaughter of the founder of Redding, the daughter of Colonel John Read, born in 1761, was Esther. If there was a reason for changing her name to Betsy, I have long since forgotten it; I suspect my brother did that for reasons of his own. There was no girlfriend in my original outline, but my brother needed a strong motivation to bring Sam back to Redding from time to time. Seventeen-year-old boys do not risk their lives to visit their mothers, he pointed out. Find a girlfriend for Sam. I found her—or Esther, at least—in the Congregational graveyard at Redding. The greatest liberty we have taken with historical fact in the entire book is making the Reads Anglicans instead of leaving them Congregationalists as they were. We did this in order to bring Timmy and Betsy together in church in a natural and frequent way. The real John Read was, in fact, a militia colonel who resigned his commission in May 1775, perhaps because of age, perhaps because of political ambivalence. His subsequent service in a civilian capacity shows, however, that he was no Tory.

Israel Putnam, a hero of the French and Indian War, but in over his head as a large strategic planner, was from the section of the northeastern Connecticut town of Pomfret which is now Brooklyn. As a commander in the disputed area north and east of New York City, he was surprised while shaving at

PHOTO BY JILL BURDEN

27

Horseneck (now Greenwich) by mounted Redcoats he spotted in his mirror. He jumped on his horse and rode, legend has it, down

a set of stone steps—several score of them—to rally his troops. This statue by Anna Huntington stands at the entrance to the Putnam Park in Redding, the site of the 1778-79 encampment. In the background are two reconstructed blockhouses and a monument to the troops who spent that bitter, hungry winter there. The oval portrait of Putnam hangs in the Connecticut State Library.

Benedict Arnold is well known. He was, in fact, one of the Governor's Second Foot Guard, and its first captain. He participated in the Battle of Danbury, as we have it here.

William Heron was in reality as we have described him. He may have been playing both sides against each other for his own political reasons, but if so, Redding residents did not perceive his role that way. Modern scholars believe he was at bottom working in the Patriot cause. After the war Heron was repeatedly elected to Redding's highest offices and represented the town in Connecticut's convention to ratify the U.S. Constitution in 1788. He voted aye. His tombstone, pictured here, stands in the little graveyard next to the Episcopal Church on Redding Ridge. The inscription reads:

"In memory of William Heron ESQ. who was born in the

PHOTO BY JILL BURDEN

28

City of Cork, Ireland, 1742 and died Jan. 8, 1819. I know that my redeemer will liveth and that he shall stand upon the [last?] day of the earth."

Jerry Sanford is an interesting case. The question of why the British would take a ten-year-old prisoner has an answer. My source for stating his age as ten was the standard history of Redding by Charles Burr Todd (p.31), a fact I checked out by looking at Jerry's gravestone in a local cemetery. Years later good friends and Redding neighbors of mine made a gravestone rubbing of the marker— shown here—and

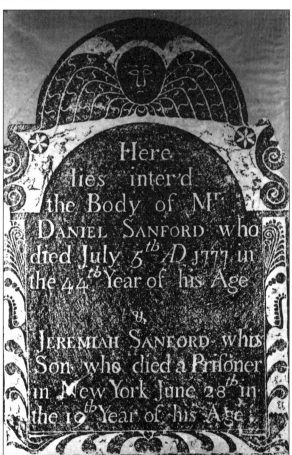

PHOTO BY LINCOLN SELLECK. COURTESY OF OLLIE SELLECK.

presented it to me. On this large sheet, what looks on cursory inspection to be a 10 turns out to be a 19—with an oversized loop. Jerry, then, wasn't an innocent child, but rather a threatening young man of prime militia age.

Tom Warrups was as we describe him. He was probably a Pootatuck, a small group that had, by the 1770s, been pretty much absorbed by the Schaghtacokes located in nearby Kent. Warrups was a local character who lived in some sort of hutlike shelter on Colonel Read's estate.

Ned is also a real person. We have him the slave of Captain Daniel Starr in whose house he was, in fact, killed. Historically, however, Ned belonged to a man named Seth Samuel Smith. During the war the General Assembly would compensate residents for property damage done by the enemy. Injured citizens could submit a petition describing the property damaged and its value, along with some sort of proof of the facts. Smith filed such materials; the originals of 1778 are still archived in the Connecticut State Library. The documents, some of which are reproduced at the end of this essay, include two eyewitness accounts of the action at Daniel Starr's house and the report by a Congregational minister, Ebenezer White, of a neighboring parish at whose house the British officers stopped for refreshment. The young officer who decapitated Ned described the whole bloody engagement to White.

The cow-boys are real. New York City was occupied throughout the war by British troops. It was surrounded on the land side by Patriot-held territory in New Jersey, Connecticut, and Westchester County. The last of these places was a veritable no-man's-land, with constant clashes between regular troops and irregular guerrillas. The major focus of activity—beyond the strategic one of commanding the Hudson River—was the collection of provisions. Legitimate livestock dealers like our Eliphalet Meeker and illegitimate land pirates called cow-boys abounded. Prices for beef were sky-high and if sold to the British could earn hard currency; if sold to the American forces would yield only depreciated Continental currency or, worse, congressional IOUs.

The Meeker family operates a tavern in a building that serves today as a private residence. This word tavern has given some teachers a small problem because today it implies a place devoted primarily to drinking alcoholic beverages. One anthologist wanted to change the word to restaurant, a French word not used by English speaking people until well into the 19th century. We compromised on inn, quite satisfactory to me since the Meeker Tavern was not only a place to eat and drink but also for overnight accommodation—and a general store, as well. (For more on our struggles with censorship, see "Censored: An Author's Perspective" at the end of this collection.) The building stands today just where we have it located—diagonally across the road from the new Episcopal Church, a replacement for Beach's structure built in 1833. It is a private dwelling today, with a breezeway and a garage. In the 1770s it would have had a rail fence instead of a stone wall. It might have had shutters, but not the louvered blinds shown here.

Literary Analysis

The political division between Whigs and Tories—Patriots and Loyalists—forms the thematic backbone of the whole story. The national anti-imperial conflict is personified in the conflict between father and son. Sam's violent and martial assertion of independence from his father is symbolized by donning a revolutionary uniform, insubordinately stealing the Brown Bess, and running away. That father and son, like English and American Englishmen, are so much alike is ironically expressed in the fact that Sam and the enemy Lobsterbacks both wear scarlet—the color, incidentally of blood.

The boy and his father are much alike: hot tempered, stubborn, and independent minded. Father, like Sam (p.51) argues with the Patriot officers come to disarm him (when, ironically, his musket is already in the hands of his Patriot son), and later Mother says (p.88): "You hate having anyone tell you what to do, . . . " And Sam, similarly in a confrontation with Mother, evinces his father's stubbornness—even to death (p.161). And we learn that Father, too, at age sixteen had run off, perhaps to enlist in the French and Indian War. (p. 88).

These similarities ironically are what lead to the men's separation. But like the revolting colonies, Sam, in Timmy's words (p. 9) "thought he was a grown up, and he didn't' want anybody to tell him what to do." The martial aspect of this conflict is suggested by   Timmy's characterization of Sam (p. 8) as "always shooting out whatever came into his mind . . . ," while father "hit Sam dozens of times. . . ." The military undertone of the father-son conflict is emphasized at the introduction of this scene when we write of the wind against the windows "making a sound like muffled drums" while "plates rattled in their racks"—like musket fire (p. 1). Children—the colonies—ought not resort to military action, but "keep a civil tongue, . . . even when they know the grownups are wrong" (pp. 8-9) Sam and Father engage in a vicarious, but bloody, battle as Father describes in gruesome detail the gory scenes of combat (p. 21). But he is defeated. "You can't order me anymore, Father, I'm a man," declares Sam. "A man? You're a boy Sam, a boy dressed up in a gaudy soldier's suit." But Father knows he has lost. "Go, Sam, Go. Get out of my sight." (p. 22) And he surrenders to tears, something Timmy has never seen before.

Sam's departure and Father's tears foreshadow the ultimate

defeat of the mother country. Timmy evinces the enormity of it when he says that this argument was "worse than the others, and it worried me that maybe they wouldn't fix it up." (p. 27)

As an aside, we should note that in a lull in the argument between Father and Sam, the Reverend John Beach—the onetime Congregational minister turned Anglican—preaches conciliation. After admonishing Sam that "God meant man to obey. He meant children to obey their fathers, he meant man to obey their Kings," Beach turns the conversation to the topic of repairs to his church —symbolically, of course, repairs to the imperial system rather than revolt against it (p. 8).

I have already alluded to the ideological elements inherent in the American struggle for national liberation. This element of the war is partly symbolized in the names Sam and Life Meeker. Sam, obviously, represents the patriotic connotation of Uncle Sam; and the pacifist father will lead a meek life. (Incidentally, I have found that few fifth graders can define the work meek. It will have to be explained to most of them.) That Father is not really so much a Loyalist as he is a pacifist is evinced in his heated lecture to Sam, "You may know principle, Sam, but I know war." (p. 21) and his tears as he accepts the inevitability of the war and Sam's part in it (p. 22). On another occasion, he says, "You never get rid of injustices by fighting." (p. 28), and Timmy correctly remarks about his father, "He's just against wars." (p. 102) Mr. Beach voices the Loyalist view that subjects should obey their king (p. 2) and "Nobody wants a rebellion except fools and hotheads." (p. 6) Sam reflects the interpretation known to historians variously as Whig, nationalist, or—after its principal 19th-century populizer— Bancroftian; perhaps it is more popularly known as the patriotic view. (This historiography is more fully explained in the essay above, "Johnny and Sam.") "It's worth dying to be free," Sam declares. The king and Parliament are "3000 miles away, how can they make laws for us?" (p. 7) However, Sam here also hints at the counterinterpretation—that of economic motivation: "Why should they get rich off our taxes back in England?" But Sam himself is being supported by Father, as Timmy points out: "He pays for you to go to Yale and sends you money for books." (p. 15) It is Father, the pacifist, who rejects the economic justification for the rebellion. "Is it worth war to save a few pence in taxes?" (p. 21) But it is not the taxes, Sam insists. "The British government is determined to keep us their slaves," he tells Timmy. But he continues, "There are principles involved, Tim. Either you live up to your principles or you don't and maybe you have to take a chance on getting killed." (pp. 34-35)

Reflecting the fact that Englishmen, and even more so Englishmen in America, were among the most free in the world in the late 18th century, Father says, "Aren't we free? The whole argument is over a few taxes that hardly amount to anything for most people. What's the use of principles if you have to be dead to keep them? ... Of course there are injustices, there are always injustices, that's the way of God's world. But you never get rid of injustices by fighting." (p. 28) This last statement is one that Sam himself would have to die to learn.

We portray the war, then, as both an anti-imperial war for national liberation and a civil war that divided a people against itself.

Timmy only episodically commits himself to either side of the argument. He sometimes admires Sam and sometimes believes that his father, the authority figure, must be right. "The way Sam explains it, he says on one occasion, "it sounds right to be a Rebel. And when Father explains it, it sounds right to be a Loyalist." (p. 103) Even the terminology had its ironic confusions, Timmy notes, for how could Rebels be Patriots? (p. 26) His early perceptions are pretty shallow, however. "I wonder," he ruminates, "if I went for a solider, which army would I join? The British had the best uniforms and the shiny new guns, but there was something exciting about the Patriots—being underdogs and fighting off the mighty British army." (p. 65) His urge to get involved was strictly nonideological. He professes his loyalty to the king when he thinks that will lead to an exciting assignment, but, he admits, "I didn't have any opinion either way ...." (pp. 75-76) Indeed, Timmy's urge to participate in the war—apparently on any side that will take him—is killed when he fails in his one opportunity to do so. After Betsy gets the best of him in a wrestling match, and the secret of his couriorship for Heron is exposed, his aspiration to heroism and glory dies. (pp. 83-84. For more on this episode, see the essay, "Censored," at the end of this collection.) From that point on, Timmy becomes a mere spectator until galvanized into action by the impending execution of Sam.

Timmy's emotional involvement deepens as events unfold, however. After Patriot militia brutalize Father and cow-boys kidnap him, Timmy declares that he suddenly realized he was a Tory. (p. 139) But within hours after watching the massacre of combatant civilians by British troops, he "didn't feel much like being a Tory anymore." (p. 145) Ultimately, Timmy commits not to the Patriots or Tories but to his father's pacifism. "It seemed to me that everybody was to blame, and I decided that I wasn't going to be on anybody's side any more. Neither one of them was right." (p. 167)

The family division, a metaphor for the division between Englishmen in England and Englishmen in America, as well as the division among Americans, tears at Timmy throughout the story. And the colonies' political and economic maturation is paralleled by Timmy's development. Out of his efforts to deal both intellectually and emotionally with the conflict between his father and his brother, Timmy comes of age.

The first glimmer of this maturity comes as Timmy is forced to take on all of Sam's chores around the tavern. Among other things, he discovers that "for some reason I suddenly got good at arithmetic." (p. 44) At one point it looks like Timmy's growth will follow the same path as Sam's. Readers might well believe so, at any event, when Timmy, outraged at Father's refusal to let him help the spy William Heron, becomes "angry enough to stand up to Father." (p. 71) But finally Timmy doesn't go that way: party because he fails in his one attempt to participate in the war, and partly because he begins to see a little deeper into Sam's motivation.

First, he challenges Sam's justification for joining the army "that all of my friends were going" (p. 58), and then much later, "I had a funny feeling about seeing Sam. It wasn't just that he was more grown up or that I was more grown up. It was something else. For the first time in my life I knew that Sam was wrong about something. I knew that I understood something better than he did." What Timmy knew was that Sam "was staying in the army because he *wanted* to stay in the army, not because of duty or anything else. He liked the excitement of it." (p. 162)

Even before this awareness hit him, Timmy had marked his intellectual growth by emulating his father rather than his brother. On the tragic trip home from Verplancks he ponders two courses of action: the daring, glorious act of hot pursuit to try to rescue Father, as Sam would have done; or the unglorious, unexciting, but arduous and ultimately more fruitful tack of getting "the oxen and the wagon load of goods back home ... so we'd have something to run the store and tavern on through the winter." (pp. 120-21) And he realizes that though not conventionally heroic, getting the goods home was the wise and right thing to do. "Ever since I had got the wagon home by myself I hadn't felt like a boy any more." (p. 132) "I wasn't acting my usual self, I was acting more like a grown up. You couldn't say that I was really an adult," the thirteen-year-old muses, "but I wasn't a child anymore, that was certain." (p. 133)

Sam represents the "patriotic" thrust toward independence, and, indeed, patriotism is one of his motives for enlisting. "Father, I am not an Englishman, I am an American, and I am going to fight to keep my country free," he says (p. 21); and on another occasion, "My duty to my country comes first." (p. 161) Sometimes, as I've already noted, Sam rises above mere national chauvinism to support his position—so damaging to his family—by principle. "It's not the money, it's the principle," he tells his father (p. 21). But he reveals other motives, too, perhaps psychologically deeper ones. He lets out that peer pressure had an effect. He couldn't stay in college, he tells Timmy, "How could I not go when all my friends were going?" (p. 58) And later when his mother and brother are in dire straits and need his help desperately, he insists on reenlisting. "We've made a promise, a group of us, not to quit until the Redcoats are beaten. We've made a pledge to each other." (p. 161)

Timmy finally sees through all Sam's rationalizations—ones that Sam probably in good faith actually believed. "He was staying the army because he *wanted* to. (p. 162) And at last, I might suggest an even deeper, perhaps most compelling reason for Sam's initial determination to go off with the army—to get way from his father. Sam had a history of running away after arguments with Father (pp. 10-11), and the bitter fight on the eve of his departure is only the worst of them (p. 22). "I'm too old for him to tell me what to do anymore," he grumbles bitterly to Timmy." (p. 33) Thus Sam, like most people, and perhaps especially adolescents, is a bundle of mixed motives, none predominating, one stronger at one moment, another at another.

The disruption of American society that both led to and accompanied the war is seen in the disruption of the Meeker family. The dilution of the medieval deference that support hierarchical social systems was a long-term trend in the English colonies, much intensified by the Great Awakening of the mid-18th century, which undermined ministerial authority. That collapse of deference is portrayed in our book principally, of course, by Sam's revolt against his father—which was, perhaps, the deepest motive for his enlisting in the Rebel cause; but it is also reflected in his mother's uncharacteristic assertiveness.

Upstairs in his loft sleeping place Timmy overhears a rare argument between his parents. His mother wants to answer Sam's letters. Father wants Sam to face life alone.

"The boy has to learn a lesson, he's far too headstrong."

"He isn't a boy anymore," Mother said.

"He's sixteen years old, that's a boy, Susannah."

"He's seventeen, Life. How old were you when you left home?"

"That was different," he growled. "There were eight of us, remember, too many mouths to feed as it was."

"Still, you went off at sixteen, Life."

"Sam's too headstrong."

"And you're not?"

"I'm his father, I don't have to be questioned on my behavior."

Mother laughed. "You hate having anyone tell you what to do, yet you expect Sam to let you order him around. I'm going to write to him, Life. He must surely be worried that we're all right."

"I don't want you to do it, Susannah."

"I know you don't, Life, but I'm going to do it anyway." (pp. 87-88)

It is no coincidence of literary construction that this female assertiveness comes just three pages after Betsy has bested Timmy in a physical struggle (pp. 83-84). Of course, Mother falls into deep depression as Sam's execution becomes inevitable and she takes to drink on occasion—a pallid reminder of a more profound alcoholism that my brother wrote into early drafts. The ending is depressing enough, I was able to persuade him; we don't need this.

Irony

As the generational conflict within the Meeker family parallels the conflict within the English-speaking empire, so does a second major theme of the story—that of irony.

This theme, established first when Sam castigates the scarlet-coated Lobsterbacks while he himself is wearing a scarlet coat (p. 2) is made explicit when Timmy says, "I thought it was pretty funny that he kept calling the British Lobsterbacks, when he was dressed in red, too." (p. 5) I have already pointed out that Sam and Father were in conflict so much because they were so much alike (especially pp. 87-88)—like the Englishmen in England and the Englishmen in America. Americans were fighting against England for what they referred to as the rights of Englishmen. This is pointed up when Timmy muses about the newspaper, *Rivington's Gazette.* "It was a Tory paper and [Father] wasn't supposed to have it; it was illegal [in Connecticut] so he kept it hidden. It made me wonder how the war was going to make us freer if you couldn't read any paper you wanted to any more." (p. 39) Historically, of course, freedom of the press was not established in England at the time, and had developed only weak beginnings in the colonies. But it was a well-understood concept among the American intelligentsia. It was the extra-constitutional Committee of Correspondence that banned *Rivington's Gazette.*

Other ironic episodes abound. Timmy lies about how the egg basket got crushed and then immediately chastises Sam, "Don't curse. It's sin." (p. 14) Timmy goes off to aid the Imperial cause whistling "Yankee Doodle," and in the same context explains that he "wanted some glory too much to be honorable." (pp. 176-77) Of course, the death of Ned, the slave, holds the central irony of the whole Revolutionary Era (p. 144). Says Sam, "The British government is determined to keep us their slaves," (p. 34) and we must risk our lives to throw off such slavery. But at the moment he spoke, more than a half a million Americans were held in slavery—thousands of them in Connecticut. Many of these—one of whom was Ned—gave their lives to gain "freedom" for their masters.

Father's death is characterized in the bitterly ironic comment he makes as he dies, "And now I go to enjoy the freedom war has brought me." (p. 165) That he dies on a British prison ship when in fact he was quite willing to aid the British is, of course, a fatal irony. It is an episode we included in order to make the point that as soon as a people get into a war, they have lost control of events. The illogical, the inexplicable—not to mention the unjust—are an inevitable result.

But none of these episodes is so profoundly ironic as Sam's

death—the culminating fact of the lesson Father points out, "In war the dead pay the debts for the living." (p. 167) The portrayal of this ghastly event is based on a couple of accounts of a pair of executions that General Israel Putnam ordered and are still invoked in the name of a place in Redding—Gallows Hill. As we explain in the back pages in "How Much of This Book is True?" two men were executed: one for stealing cattle and another, John Smith, for insubordination. Smith was a seventeen-year-old deserter from the British army now a Rebel private disaffected and preaching desertion to his fellows in camp at Redding. It was Smith whose clothing caught fire and smoldered as he lay writhing in his last agony. That Sam's death came at the hands of his own troops for stealing his own cattle that, in fact, he didn't steal is a complex of ironies that bring a fatal close to *My Brother Sam Is Dead.*

Historical Miscellany

In 1775 when our story begins, most Americans had not sorted themselves out as Whigs or Tories. This was not so much the case in Connecticut, however. Here the parliamentary act of 1765 that imposed taxes on the use of certain documents, an act that affected colonists everywhere divided the colony deeply and bitterly, unlike the early imperial measures that burdened coastal merchants and land speculators principally. Sides were taken then, and in subsequent elections the fiercest opponents of the Stamp Act came to dominate colony politics and government.

Sam would have been a five-year-old child in 1765, growing up in a politically uninvolved family—a situation perhaps determined by Father's need to stay out of controversy for fear of alienating customers. But as a sixteen-year-old at Yale he would have found himself buried in a hotbed of Whiggery—especially of the ideological kind. I should note, since it is a question school kids raise, that entrance to Yale depended on a reading knowledge of

Latin and Greek and not much else. These languages were customarily mastered by the clergy, who prepared local boys for college. Youths as young as thirteen were enrolled at Yale.

Sam has enlisted, along with numerous college friends, including Aaron Burr and Ethan Allen, in the Second Foot Guard, a militia company organized in 1774 by Benedict Arnold, a local apothecary and Caribbean merchant. Arnold has designed the uniforms which looked as we describe them (p. 2). The Lexington Alarm brought militia troops from all over New England to the outskirts of Boston. The famous "shot heard 'round the world" that Sam tells about raises the question of who fired first. That has been a matter of investigation and controversy ever since April 20, 1775. In 1994 historian David Hackett Fischer, in the most thorough and best-considered assessment of the situation, concludes, "We shall never know who fired first at Lexington." Sam's description of "some church steeple in Boston" (p. 4) of course refers to the Old North Church, Anglican and shut up because of the unpopularity of its minister. Here in the deserted church, the tallest building in Boston, Paul Revere's coconspirators climbed to the topmost window in the steeple and held out two tiny lanterns. Sam goes on then to give his fragmentary account of the battles at Lexington, Concord, and the roadway back to Boston. Sam rejoins his company in New Haven; they march one hundred forty miles and arrive at Cambridge on April 29.

Though all New England men of militia age were required to have guns, many did not; and many weapons at hand were in bad repair. Most were left over from service in the French and Indian War and had seen no fighting since 1761. These were government issue muskets fired when a piece of flint activated by the trigger struck a piece of steel and sent a spark into a pan of powder, and thus were called flintlocks. They were smooth bored—no rifling—and fired a bullet of about .75 caliber, that is about three-quarters of an inch in diameter. The barrel was forty-six inches long, and with the wooden stock, the weapon was about five feet long and a twenty-inch bayonet was attached during combat. The model pictured here is four feet, ten inches long.

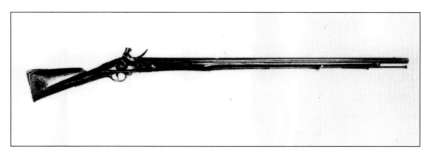

The length of the weapon became a matter of concern for the artist who drew the dust jacket for the first edition and still encloses the hardcover (Simon & Schuster) edition. The illustration shows Sam running across a field holding the weapon across his body (described on pp. 59-60). The proportions were such that either the Brown Bess was much too long or Sam was a real shrimp. My agreement with our publishers gives me approval of the artwork in matters of historical accuracy. I sent it back, and the artist redrew the musket.

Earlier military muskets used by the British had black stocks. The version Sam used was introduced in the 1740s and the stocks were painted brown. Also, the barrels, which were shiny when manufacturerd, were burnished so they would not pick up a glint in the sun. One of these conditions probably provided the word brown. Bess may have come from Queen Elizabeth, during whose reign a much earlier version was introduced; or perhaps from a corruption of buchse, or busche, the German word for gun. And then there are those who claim the term Brown Bess was not used at all until after 1780. The general description of the musket and its use around New England farms given by Timmy (p. 18) is accurate.

NOTE: It was customary in the 18th century and well into the next one for people to share beds. Perfect strangers expected to sleep two or three to a bed when traveling; and within families it was a matter of course. Though normally the sexes were separated, cases of both sexes sharing beds were not unknown, especially among the servant class.

In the era before the temperance movement of the 1820s and 1830s, Americans consumed a great deal more alcohol than they do today. Daily grog was an expectation of all classes, that is, water laced with rum or whiskey—to purify it if for no other reason. In New England rum and cider were the drinks of the common man. Cider was fermented and brought to about 10 percent alcohol to be "hard"—apple wine really.

Sam's Military Service

Sam served in Washington's command during the siege of Boston, and when the British evacuated the city, because of his knowledge of the source of provisions—especially livestock—in western Connecticut, he was assigned to Captain (later Colonel) Henry Champion, the commissary officer for the region. This gets him down into the Redding neighborhood and permits him to visit Betsy and make contact with his family.

THESE PICTURES, TAKEN IN 1998, SHOW THE MONUMENTS ERECTED NEAR THE SITE OF THE BRITISH INVASION OF APRIL 25, 1777 AT COMPO BEACH IN NORWALK, NOW WESTPORT, CONNECTICUT.

The next time we hear of Sam's whereabouts he is briefly at Horseneck (present-day downtown Greenwich) near the New York line (p. 80). He returns to Redding with a mixed force of militia and Continentals under Generals David Wooster and Benedict Arnold, who came on the heels of the British troops invading the Connecticut countryside on their way to burn military supplies stored at Danbury, a

twenty-five-mile march from Long Island Sound, and about ten miles north of Redding. The British had landed at what is now Compo Beach in Westport, which in 1777 was part of Norwalk. I should note that research subsequent to the publication of the first edition of *Brother Sam* showed that my map of the British trek was inaccurate. That map has the troops reembarking at Calf Pasture in Norwalk. Later paperback editions have a corrected map showing the troops leaving from the same point at which they began the invasion. The hardcover edition still includes the inaccurate map.

The Danbury invasion is one of the few inland incursions by the British in New England, and a classic amphibious operation. It was intended to divert Continental troops from operations in the Highlands around West Point and south of New York City, as well as to destroy the Continental magazine in Danbury. Much important materiel was destroyed and the troops burned nineteen houses and twenty-two barns in Danbury and mortally wounded General Wooster in Ridgefield. On their return through Ridgefield and Wilton Parish the British troops were peppered from behind stone walls and trees in an engagement reminiscent of the march from Concord to Boston, and lost about two hundred men. American losses, in addition to the valuable supplies and other property such as Daniel Starr's house and Seth Smith's slave, were about twenty killed and forty wounded.

Sam's next return to Redding is his ill-fated duty with Israel Putnam's command in winter quarters in 1778-79, an operation often referred to as the second Valley Forge because of the similarity of cold, starvation, and general deprivation. Putnam's fame rested on actions during the French and Indian War. He was a commanding field officer, but lacked the breadth of intelligence for strategic planning. He had failed Washington in the Battle of New York and subsequently he was given command in less demanding situations. In 1778 he was sixty years old and overweight. A year later he would suffer a stroke, forcing him to retire from active service; he died in 1790. He was hard-bitten and quite capable of the actions we portray, portrayals based on actual events. Sam's military career, then, extended from April 1776 to his execution on February 6, 1779.

This picture, drawn in the 1830s, shows a house that well-supported local tradition tells us was the Redding headquarters of General Israel Putnam during the bitter winter of 1778-79. It was torn

GENERAL PUTNAM'S REDDING HEADQUARTERS

down sometime toward the middle of the 19th century.

Shown here, also, is a reconstruction of one of the cabins—about two hundred of them—that housed troops at the Redding

PHOTO BY JILL BURDEN

encampment, now Putnam Park. In 1974 there were several reconstructed cabins for enlisted men; they have been allowed to decay to nothing, and all that remains is this one that housed officers.

Bibliography

Buel, Richard, Jr. *Dear Liberty: Connecticut's Mobilization for the Revolutionary War.* Middletown, Conn.: Wesleyan University Press, 1980.

Collier, Christopher. *Roger Sherman's Connecticut: Yankee Politics and the American Revolution.* Middletown, Conn.: Wesleyan University Press, 1971.

_____. and James L. Collier, *The American Revolution, 1763-1783.* Tarrytown, N.Y.: Marshall Cavendish, 1998.

Connecticut. *The Public Records of the Colony of Connecticut.* Volume 15. 1775-1776. Charles J. Hoadley, ed. Hartford, Case, Lockwood & Branaird, 1890.

Connecticut. *The Public Records of the State of Connecticut.* Volume 1. 1776-1778. Charles J. Hoadley, ed. Hartford, Case, Lockwood & Branaird, 1894.

Destler, Chester M. *Connecticut: The Provisions State.* Chester, Conn.: The Pequot Press, 1973.

Jones, Gwynfor. "An Early Amphibious Operation; Danbury, 1777," *Journal of the Society for Army Historical Research*, 46 (Autumn 1968): 187.

Main, Jackson Turner. *Connecticut Society in the Era of the American Revolution.* Hartford, Conn.: American Revolution Bicentennial Commission of Connecticut, 1977.

McDevitt, Robert. *Connecticut Attacked: A British Viewpoint, Tryon's Raid on Danbury.* Chester, Conn.: Pequot Press, 1974. This is the work that corrects the map of Tryon's troops' march erroneously depicted in Ward below.

Niven, John. *Connecticut Hero: Israel Putnam.* Hartford, Conn.: American Revolution Bicentennial Commission of Connecticut, 1977.

Prendergast, William J. (comp.). *Two Hundred Years: The Second Company Governor's Foot Guard, 1775-1975.* Deep River, Conn.: New Era Publishing Company, 1975.

Steiner, Bruce E. *Connecticut Anglicans in the Revolutionary Era: A Study in Communal Tensions.* Hartford, Conn.: American Revolution Bicentennial Commission of Connecticut, 1978.

Todd, Charles Burr. *The History of Redding, Connecticut.* Newburgh, N.Y.: Newburgh Journal Company, 1906.

Van Dusen, Albert E. *Connecticut.* New York: Random House, 1961.

Ward, Christopher. *The War of the Revolution.* Ed. by John Richard Alden. New York: The Macmillan Company, 1952. This includes a very brief account of the Danbury raid, but has the reembarkation point of the British troops wrong.

Zeichner, Oscar. *Connecticut's Years of Controversy, 1750-1776.* Chapel Hill: University of North Carolina Press, 1949.

Documents: The Decapitation of Ned

The Connecticut General Assembly permitted Patriots whose property was destroyed by enemy action to petition for compensation. One such petitioner was Seth Samuel Smith, the owner of a slave named Ned. In order to prove that Ned belonged to Smith, that he was worth eighty pounds, and that he was destroyed by the British, Smith found three people to testify to the events.

Two of them were Anna and Ebenezer Weed—relationship unknown—who viewed the action from a house across the road, the view that our fictional Timmy would have from behind a stone wall. The other deponent was Ebenezer White, a Congregational minister from whom the British officers demanded food and drink just after the episode.

It was customary for aristocratic fathers in England to buy commissions for their younger sons—often at ages as young as fifteen. We do not know how old the Earl of Fakland's son was, but he was probably not over twenty. I say this because he must have been a very junior officer to have actually led a squad into the action.

The Earl of Fakland's son—and we have no better appellation for him than that—may have enhanced his story: A teenager having just experienced probably the most exciting moment of his life, perhaps with a glass or two of wine or a mug of grog under his belt, might be expected to exaggerate. But his fellow officers, "a number of gentlemen," were with him, so I believe his story. Certainly I accept the accuracy and veracity of the Reverend Mr. White's account.

The game I play with students is to ask if we have eyewitnesses to the action; we do—the Weeds. Do we have eyewitnesses to the decapitation of Ned? We do not—we have only White's hearsay report. As a historian, I find Falkland's story credible. But as a jury member, I don't think I would find that he killed Ned "beyond a reasonable doubt." What do your students think?

It might be necessary to draw out from your students the legal fact that Ned was property. They might also be asked to discover for themselves from a careful reading that Mr. White was a minister. Note that these depositions were given eight months after the event, so memory may not have been fresh. All the depositions are written in the same hand, which tells us that either they were copied for submission to the Assembly or that they were given orally and taken down by a single interviewer.

The Petition of S.S. Smith Re: The Death of Ned

*Transcribed from the original manuscripts at the Connecticut
State Library by Christopher Collier*

To the Hon^bl [Honorable] General Assembly now sitting by adj^t
[adjournment] at Hartford in and for the State of Connecticut. —

The petition of Sam^ll Smith of Reading in Fairfield County humbly
showeth —

That on or about the 26th day of april last past your Petitioner
owned and was possessed as of his own proper estate a negro man
named Ned a slave for life well worth eighty pounds lawful
money and when the enemy of the united States of American
made their excursion into the Country to Danbury and s^d [said]
Negro being a very Zealous friend to the American cause turned
out and went to Danbury to oppose the British Troops and then
and there bravely fought and opposed s^d Troops till he was killed
by the s^d Enemies, Your Petitioner therefore having received no
satisfaction for the loss of s^d Negoro, and looking upon him to be
as much and as really his your Petitioner's property as tho' it had
been a house or any other valuable article that was then & there
Destroyed by s^d Troops prays your Honours to order the Treasurer
of this State to pay to your Petitioner the value of s^d Negro man
out of the Treasurery or in some other way as you in your great
wisdome shall judge best grant relief to your Petitioner in the
Premises and your Petitioner as in duty bound shall ever pray
                    Samuel Smith
Redding Jany 21st 1778

Ebenezer White of Danbury of Lawful Age Testifies and says that
on or About the 26th Day of April 1777 at Evening there Being A
Number of Gentlemen at his House Belonging to the British Army
Amongst which, was one, whom he understood was the Earl of

Falklands Son Who told him (the Deponent) that he was the first
that Entered Maj^r Starrs House & found A Number of men in S^d
House Amongst which was two Negro's all which they Instantly
Killed & Set Fire to the House Giving this for A Reason why they
Did so that it was their Constant Practice where they found peo-
ple Shut up in a House & firing upon them to kill them & burn

Ebenezer White of Danbury of Lawful Age testifies and Says 231 a
that on or about the 26th day of April 1777 at Evening there
Being a Number of Gentlemen at his House Belonging to
British Army Amongst which, was one, whom he understood
the Earl of Falklands Son Who told him (the deponent)
he was the first that Entred Majr. Starrs House & found a Number
of men in sd. House Amongst which was two Negros at which
they Instantly Skilled & Set fire to the House Giving this for
a Reason Why they did So that it was their Constant Practice
where they found People Shut up in a House & firing upon them
they made it a Practice to kill them & burn the house & further the
Deponent Saith that the aforesaid Young Gentlemen told him that one
of the aforesaid Negros after he had run him through, tore up &
attempted to Shoot him & that he the aforesaid Earl of Falklands Son
Cut his head off himself, which Negro the deponent hath under-
=stood Since was the Property of Mr. Saml. Smith of Reading
And further the deponent Saith not

Danbury Janry 26th 1778 then the Revd. Mr. Eben. White the above
Named Deponent Personally appearing made oath to the Truth of
the above written Disposition Sworn to before me Thad. Benedict Justice of the

Ebenezer Weed of Danbury of Lawful Age testifies & Says that on or about
the 26 th day of April 1777 he being at home across the road opposite to
Majr. Daniel Starrs house he See a Negro at sd. House which he knew to be
the Property of Mr. Saml. Smith of Reading about a half hour as near as
he can judge before the british Troops came to sd. House & further the
deponent Saith that in the Evening of sd. day he heard a man belonging to
the british Army Say that they had Skilled one damd Black with the white
in sd. Starrs House and Further the deponent Saith not.

Danbury Janry 26th 1778 then Ebenr. Weed the above Named
Deponent Personally appearing made oath to ye Truth of the foregoing
Disposition Sworn before me Thad. Benedict Justice of Peace

Anna Weed of Danbury of Lawful age testifies & Says that on or about
the 26 th day of April 1777 She being at home across the road opposite
to Majr. Starrs House She See a Negro at sd. house which She understood
was the Property of Mr. Saml. Smith of Reading but a Short time before
the british Troops came up to sd. House & further the deponent Saith
She heard one of the british Soldiers Say here is a damd. black in the
house what shall we do with him another answered Damn him
Skill him & Immediately the House was in flames & further the deponent
Saith not.

Danbury Janry 26th 1778 then Anna Weed the above named
Deponent Personally appearing made oath to ye Truth of
above written Disposition Sworn to before me Tho.

the house & further the Deponnent Saith that the aforesaid Young
Gentleman told him that one of the aforesaid Negro's after he had
Run him through Rose up & Attempted to shoot him & that he
the aforesaid Earl of Falklands Son Cut his head off himself,
which Negro the Deponent hath understood since was the
Property of Mr. Sam¹ Smith of Redding.

And further the Deponent Saith not Danbury Janʸ 26ᵗʰ 1778 then
the Revᵈ Mr. Ebenʳ White the above Named Deponant Personally
appearing made oath to the Truth of the above written Deposition
Sworn to before me Thadᵘˢ Benedict Justic of Pc

Ebenezer Weed of Danbury of Lawful Age Testifies & Says that on
or about the 26th Day of April 1777 he being at home across the
Road opposite to Majʳ Daniel Starrs house he See a Negro at Sᵈ
House which he knew to be the Property of Mʳ Sam¹ Smith of
Redding about a half hour as near as he can judge Before the
British Troops came to Sᵈ House & further the Deponent Saith
that in the Evening of Sᵈ Day he heard A man Belonging to the
British Army Say that they had killed one Dam'd Black with the
white in Sᵈ Starrs House and Further the Deponent Saith not —
Danbury Janʸ 26th 1778 then Ebenʳ Weed the above Named
Deponent Personally appearing made oath to yᵉ Truth of the fore-
going Deposition Sworn before me Thadᵘˢ Benedict Justice of
Peace

Anna Weed of Danbury of Lawful Age Testifies & Says that on or
about the 26th Day of April 1777 She being at home across the
Road opposite to Majʳ Starrs House She See a Negro at Sᵈ house
which She understood was the Property of Mʳ Sam¹ Smith of
Reading but a Short time before the British Troops came up to Sᵈ
House & further the Deponent Saith She heard one of the British
Soldiers Say here is a Dam'd Black in the House what Shall we Do
with him, another answer'd Damn him Kill him & Imediately the
House was in flams & further the Deponent Saith not

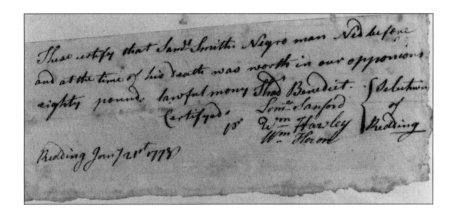

Danbury Jan[y] 1778 then Anna Weed the above named Deponent Personally appearing made oath to y[e] Truth of the above written Deposition Swarn to before me
Thad[us] Benedict Justice of Peace

Play. 1775: A Family Chooses Sides

This playlet, an adaptation made in 1975 for subscribers to Scholastic's *JS*, and reprinted here with permission, is included for noncommercial classroom use. It focuses on the division in the Meeker family over the necessity for combat and provides at least three perspectives: Father's pacifism; Mr. Beach's Loyalism; and Sam's Patriotism. It portrays the family division as a metaphor for divisions both among Americans and between Americans and Parliament. It raises, as well, the problem of the conflict between loyalty and patriotism.

1775: A Family Chooses Sides

(From *JS: Junior Scholastic.* September 23, 1975. Reprinted with permission.)

Characters

Father (Eliphalet Meeker), an innkeeper
Mother (Susannah Meeker)
Sam Meeker, 16, student at Yale
Tim Meeker, 12, schoolboy
Farmer and Wife
Mr. Beach, Anglican minister

ACT I

(The Meeker residence, main room. The house is partly a store and partly an inn. On back wall is a huge stone fireplace. A hunting musket hangs over the mantel. Center, a big wooden table with benches. On walls are barrels and containers of merchandise: nails, salt and flour, some tools, pots and pans. Door stage left leads to kitchen. Door upstage left to upstairs bedrooms. Door stage right is front door. Stool upstage left. Since Tim is also the narrator, he will alternate between the stool and action center stage. At curtain, the following are seated at table, eating supper: Father, Mother, Tim, Mr. Beach, a farmer and his wife.)

Farmer *(eating)*: Venison?

Mother: Venison stew.

Farmer's Wife: It's very good.

Beach: Excellent.

Farmer: Much deer this winter?

Father: Not bad.

Farmer *(nodding to gun over fireplace)*: Brown Bess, isn't it?

54

Father (*rises, goes to fireplace, takes down gun*): Belonged to my grandfather. It's almost a family heirloom. (*He sights along it.*) Got a lot of deer with this. (*Thinks.*) Some Frenchmen, too.

Farmer: You at Louisbourg? (*Father nods.*) Lot of good men fought at Louisbourg, or so I hear.

Farmer's Wife: The Widow Matthews down the way is always talking about her son Johnny. He fought at Louisbourg.

Father: Johnny was my best friend. (*Thinks.*) We went off together, you know, full of vinegar! Oh, were we proud. Fighting with His Majesty's best! Oh, were we gonna give it to those French! A real war! (*Looks at gun, shakes his head, puts gun back over fireplace.*) But it's not fun, war. There must be a better way to settle things.

Tim: Could I have some more stew, Mother, please?

Mother: Anyone else? Mr. Beach?

Beach: If it's not too much to— (*The door slams open and bangs against the wall. Sam stands in the doorway, wearing a wet red uniform.*)

Sam: We've beaten the British in Massachusetts! We've—

Father: Shut the door! The rain is blowing in.

Sam (*shuts door*): We've done it! We've beaten the British in Massachusetts!

Father: *Who* has beaten the British?

Sam: *We* have! The Patriots!

Father: I think we're all patriots here.

Sam: All right, then. The *Minutemen*. The Minutemen have beaten the British! The Lobsterbacks marched out of Boston yesterday, looking for Mr. Adams and Mr. Hancock. When the British got to Lexington, the Lexington Minutemen tried to stop them there in the square. But there were too many British, and they pushed their way up to Concord looking for the Patriot ammunition supply.

Beach: Are you referring, Sam to the *rebel* ammunition supply?

Sam: I mean, sir, the — the *American* ammunition supply.

Beach: I do believe we're all Americans here, and all patriots.

Sam: Patriots are people who take arms against the King!

Father: Don't talk back!

Sam: Sorry, Mr. Beach. The Concord Minutemen were able to hid most of the ammunition, so the British didn't find much. And then when they turned around and went back, the Minutemen hid in the fields across the road and massacred them all the way back to Boston. (*Pause. The others are shocked into silence.*) I'm starved. (*Sits at table.*) I started out from Yale this early morn. Haven't eaten since. (*Mother gets up, fills a plate with stew from iron pot on fire and sets the food before Sam. He bends over the plate, eating wolfishly.*)

Father: Don't eat like that! (*Sam, embarrassed, sits up straight, eats more slowly.*)

Father: All right now. Tell us the news again—and in an orderly manner.

Sam: Well, it's hard to tell it orderly, Father. There were so many rumors around New Haven last night that—

Father: I thought so. Rumors!

Sam: No, no! It's true about the fighting. Captain Arnold told us himself.

Father: Captain Arnold?

Sam: Captain Benedict Arnold. He's Captain of the Governor's Second Foot Company. (*Sam looks down at his plate, then up again.*) That's my company.

Father: I guess that explains the fancy clothes.

Sam: Captain Arnold designed the uniform himself.

Father: Never mind that. Now, about that battle at Lexington. There's one thing you haven't told us. Who shot first?

Sam: Well, the British. I mean, that's what they said ....

Beach: Who said?

Sam: Well, I'm not sure. It's hard to tell in a battle. But anyway—

Father: Sam. Who do you think fired first?

Sam: I don't know, Father, I don't know. But anyway—

Father: I think it might be important to know that, Sam.

Sam (*getting angry*): Why does that matter? What right have the Lobsterbacks to be here anyway? (*Tim snickers.*) What are you laughing at?

Tim: You. You're all in red yourself.

Sam: There's a difference!

Farmer: What happened in Massachusetts is rebellion! Those blasted Sons o' Liberty will have us in a war yet!

Beach: No, I don't think so. War's just the wish of a few idiots in Boston. I think men of common sense will prevail. Nobody wants rebellion except fools and hotheads.

Sam: That's not what they say in New Haven, sir. They say that the whole colony of Massachusetts is ready to fight. And if Massachusetts fights, Connecticut will fight, too.

Father (*slams fist on table; the plates jump*): I will not have treason spoken in my house, Sam!

Sam: Father, that isn't treason!

Father (*raises his fist*): In my house I will decide what constitutes treason!

Beach: I don't think the people of Redding an anxious to fight, Sam.

Sam: You get the wrong idea from Redding, sir. A lot of people in this area are loyal to the King. But you won't find so many in the rest of the colonies.

Beach: Now, Sam. I think you'll find that loyalty is a virtue everywhere you go. We've had these things before. Take that nonsense about the tea! A bunch of madmen dressed up like

Indians and throwing tea into Boston Harbor! These agitators—
these so-called Sons of Liberty—they always manage to stir up the
passions of the people, but it never lasts. A week later, or a month
later, everybody's forgotten it—

Mother: Except the wives and children of the men who've been
killed.

Sam (*silent a moment, then to Beach*): Sir, I think it's worth dying
to be free.

Father (*standing angrily*): Free? Free to do what, Sam? Free to
mock your King? To shoot your neighbors? To make a mess of
thousands of lives?

Sam: You don't understand, Father. If the British won't let us be
free, we have to fight. Why should they get rich off our taxes back
in Britain? They're 3,000 miles away. How can they possibly
make laws for us? They have no idea at all of how things are here.
What's more, they don't care.

Beach: God meant man to obey. He meant children to obey their
fathers, he meant men to obey their kings. Answer me this, Sam.
Do you really think you know better than the King and those
learned men in Parliament?

Sam: Some of those men in Parliament agree with me, sir.

Beach: Not many, Sam.

Sam: Edmund Burke? Edmund Burke says—

Father: There'll be no more talk about this tonight!

Mother (*in back of Sam, puts her hands on his shoulders*): Sam, Sam.

59

Sam isn't rebellious. Sam's just too quick with his tongue. Aren't you Sam? If only Sam would learn to stop and think before he spoke. *(She glances at others, then at Father.)* But of course, Sam comes by it—naturally. Don't you Sam? *(Gives his hair a friendly tug.)* After all, Sam is just a chip off the old block. *(Sam smiles slightly; Father gives a good-natured snort.)*

Father: Certain ornery children should be seen and not heard.

Sam *(quietly)*: I'm not a child. I'm 16. I've been away at college almost a year.

Father: Sam, you've got yourself a nice uniform with nice shiny silver buttons. But when it comes to war, you're a babe in the woods. I've been in a war. I know. I remember friends with holes in their chest. War is not a game, Sam. People get killed.

Curtain

ACT II

(The scene begins with Tim seated on a stool. Rest of stage is darkened.)

Tim: Both Sam and my father had pretty hot tempers, as you've seen. At it always scared me when Sam argued with grown-ups like that, though I expect my father was right. Children are supposed to keep quiet and not say anything, even when they know grown-ups are wrong. But it's not always easy. Especially for Sam, who was a great debater, and always talking about the "telling points" he won in his debates at college. He used to boast to me about it. Of course, he never dared to boast to grown-ups, 'cause boasting is caused by pride. And pride is a sin. Anyway, after supper, I went out to the barn and started milking old Pru—she's our cow—and I was just about finished when Sam showed.

(Scene shifts to a stall in the barn. When lights go up, Tim is seated on a milking stool, milking the cow.)

Tim: 'Bout time. You gonna help me?

Sam: I wasn't going to but Mother said that the Devil finds use for idle hands.

Tim: You can start by pitching some hay.

Sam: I'll get my uniform all dirty. *(He sits down.)*

Tim: Thanks *a lot*. Listen, Sam. Why do you always have to get into a fight with Father?

Sam: Why does he always have to pick a fight with me?

Tim: You're not being fair. If it weren't for him, you wouldn't be at college. He pays for you. He sends you money for books. You *knew* he wouldn't like it when he saw you in that uniform.

Sam: Suppose I told you I had to wear this uniform for a reason.

Tim: I don't believe it!

Sam: It's true. I'm going to fight the Lobsterbacks.

Tim: I don't believe it! You're just trying to show off!

Sam: Oh, you'll believe it soon enough. Tomorrow I'm walking up to Wethersfield to meet my company. Then we're goin' to Massachusetts to fight the Lobsterbacks. *(Pause. He shouts:)* The Lobsterbacks! *(He laughs.)*

Tim: Won't you be scared?

Sam: Captain Arnold says it's all right to be scared. He's a brave man. He'll lead us through the Lobsterbacks like a hot knife through butter.

Tim: Sam, why did you come home?

Sam (*hesitates*): I can't tell you.

Tim: Why not?

Sam: You'll tell father.

Tim: I won't. I swear I don't.

Sam: Yes, you will.

Tim: All right, then, don't tell me. I don't care. Why, I don't believe any of it anyway.

Sam: Will you promise you won't tell?

Tim: I swear. On my honor.

Sam: This is serious, Tim.

Tim: I swear on my honor.

Sam (*takes a deep breath*): I've come for the gun. I've come to get the Brown Bess. (*Tim is shocked. His mouth falls open in dismay.*)

Tim: Sam, you can't!

Sam: I told you it was serious.

Tim: Father'll kill you.

Sam: If I don't have that gun, some Lobsterback will kill *me*. Besides, it belongs to the family. I have as much right to it as anyone.

Tim: That gun belongs to Father!

Sam: You swore, Timmy. You took an oath.

(Lights fade. Tim returns to stool.)

Tim: Of course, I sure wish I hadn't made that promise. Father needed that gun for protection against wolves and robbers. Guns were mighty important, and they weren't easy to come by. So I went back to the house, said goodnight, and went to bed. I was pretty tired. And I fell right asleep. Shouting woke me up. Sam and Father were arguing. *(Light on center stage.)*

Father: You are not going to have that gun! You are not going to Wethersfield! And you are going to take that uniform off right now, even if you have to go to church tomorrow naked!

Sam: Father—

Father: I will not have rebellion under my very own roof! We are Englishmen. We are subjects of the King. This rebellion is the talk of madmen!

Sam: Father, I am not an Englishmen. I'm an American! And I am going to fight to keep my country free!

Father: Fight? Just what are you talking about? Is it worth a war to save a few pennies in taxes?

Sam: It's not the money! It's the principle of the thing!

Father: Principle? Oh, Sam! You may know principle, but I know war! Have you ever seen a dead friend lying in the grass with the top of his head blown off? Have you ever heard a man scream when a bayonet went through him? I have, Sam. I have. I was at the battle of Louisbourg years before you were born. Oh, it was a great victory! They celebrated it with bonfires all over the colonies! And I had to carry the body of my best friend Johnny Matthews back home to his mother—in a sack. You want to come home that way? You think I want to hear a wagon draw up some fine summer morning, a morning when all the birds are singing, and your mother is so happy? And then have to go out and find you lying dead on that wagon? It isn't worth it, Sam. Now take off that uniform and get back to your studies.

Sam: I can't, Father.

Father: Sam, I'm ordering you!

Sam: You can't order me anymore, Father. I'm a man.

Father: A man? You're a boy! A little boy playing soldier, dressed up in a flashy uniform.

Sam: But Father—

Father: Get out! Get out of my sight! I can't bear to look at you anymore! Dressed up in that vile uniform! So get out! And don't come back until you can come dressed as my son, and not as a stranger.

Sam: Please—

Father: Go.

(Lights out center stage. Spotlight on Tim, seated on stool.)

Tim: There were other sounds. Then the door slammed. Then I heard some strange sounds. Sounds I'd never heard before. They puzzled me. So I eased my way down the stairs, one at a time, till I could see into the room. Father had his head down on the table, between his arms. And he was crying. I'd never seen him cry before in my whole life. I knew there were bad times coming.

Curtain

ACT III

(The scene opens with Tim seated on stool. Rest of stage is dark.)

Tim: Sam left home after that, and took the Brown Bess with him. We didn't know where he went. Now that he had a gun we figured he'd done what he planned to do—join the Patriots and fight the British. But we didn't hear from him. In fact, we didn't hear much about the war.

It's a funny thing. You'd think that if there was a war going on, it would change everything and make your life different. But our life was pretty normal. Of course, we did hear about battles. There was Bunker Hill in June of 1775. I guess the Patriots lost that one, though they killed a lot of British. But these battles seemed a long way away, and our life went on as before. I did see quite a bit of Betsy Read, though. She was Sam's girlfriend, and after Sam left, she came to the in quite a lot ... *(Light fades on Tim.)*

Mother: Hello, Betsy. How's your family?

Betsy: In good health, thank you.

Mother: I expect you've come for something. What do you need?

Betsy: Mother sent me for some cotton thread.

Mother: Tim, could you get some thread for Betsy? I have to see how dinner is coming along. *(She exits to kitchen.)*

Tim: Betsy, have you heard from Sam?

Betsy: No ... nothing. *(Pause.)* Tim, are you on you father's side or Sam's?

Tim *(uncomfortably)*: I don't know ... I don't understand what the war is all about. What side is your family on, Betsy?

Betsy: Oh, we're all Patriots. After all, my grandfather is head of the militia here in town.

Tim: Is your father going to fight the Lobsterbacks?

Betsy: I don't think so. He's too old. Anyway he doesn't think we ought to fight unless we really have to. He says there ought to be *some* way of working it out with the King and Parliament without having to fight.

Tim: That's what my father says. Only he thinks that taking arms against the King is *treason.*

Betsy: Well, there are times when you have to fight for what you believe is right.

Tim: I guess so. But who wants to get killed?

Betsy: Sometimes you have to stand up for your principles.

Tim: But Betsy, *you* don't have to take a chance of getting killed.

Betsy: I'd fight if I could. Tim, you could help us by keeping an ear out here at the inn. With all the Tories around Redding there'll be lots of talk about what the British are up to. You could find out who the Tories are—who's on our side and things like that.

Tim (*nervously*): I don't think I'd hear anything like that. Mother and Father keep me pretty busy with the chores.

Mother (*re-entering room*): Betsy, I don't think your mother intended for you to spend the day idling.

Betsy: Yes, I must be going. (*To Tim*) Think about what I said, Tim. (*She exits.*)

Mother: Tim, it's getting late. We might have guests for dinner. Will you help me set the table?

Tim: Yes, Mother. (*Tim starts to set the table.*)

Mrs. Smith (*enters, very upset*): Is Mr. Meeker here?

Mother: What's happened, Mrs. Smith?

Mrs. Smith: I went out this afternoon to bring the cows in for milking, and they were gone! Soldiers must have taken them! Whenever soldiers need food they just help themselves to other people's cattle, without paying for them. But what am I supposed to do without my milking cows? No milk, no butter, no cheese. I'm ruined!

Mother: I'm so sorry Mrs. Smith —

Mrs. Smith: I thought you or Mr. Meeker might have known if troops had passed through town yesterday —

Mother: I think I do remember troops passing by. But I paid no mind, it being near meal time, and so much to do. My husband is up in the woodlot, now. But I'll ask Mr. Meeker when he comes back, and let you know.

Mrs. Smith: Thank you ... I don't suppose it will do any good to complain to the authorities. But I just don't know what I'll do without my milking cows. Oh, these are terrible times! *(She exits.)*

Mother: I feel so sorry for her. She made her living from those milking cows. Oh, these times! Timmy ... I think we have some customers. Hurry now, and finish setting the table!

(Travelers, men and women, enter.)

Traveler *(enters with wife)*: Hello! Might we get a bite to eat?

Mother: Yes, come in. Sit right here *(motions to place at table)*. Timmy, will you bring these good people their dinner?

Tim: Yes, Mother.

Mother: Did you have a good journey?

Traveler's Wife: The road is so dusty ... we're just covered with dust!

(Father enters carrying wood for fireplace.)

Mother: Will you be going on?

Traveler's Wife: Yes, I expect we'll be traveling until 10 tonight. Then it's up at three in the morning to start again. We've been three days traveling from Boston.

Tim (*placing food on table*): You're from Boston?

Traveler's Wife: Yes, have you been there?

Tim: No, but my brother Sam was heading that way to fight the

Mother: Timmy — (*She motions for him to hush as Father's face flushes with anger.*)

Traveler: I doubt that your brother has seen much action. It's been quiet since the Battle of Bunker Hill in June. Both sides are just staying put, training, drilling. General Washington has quite a job on his hands, trying to turn that motley band of his into a real army.

Second Traveler: I don't give him much of a chance. He's got only half as many men as the British. I think we're fools to take up arms against the British!

Second Traveler's Wife: I don't understand why we can't settle these differences with Britain peacefully. The colonies do not wish to be independent. We only say that Parliament does not have the right to tax us. Let King George ask the colonial legislatures for taxes. I'm sure we would give the King whatever he pleases if he would only ask.

Third Traveler: The King's not to blame — it's his advisers who are responsible for the trouble we're in. If King George would only realize that Lord North and the other ministers are giving him bad advice.

Fourth Traveler: Those are foolish hopes. Britain is not going to give in. And neither should we! We must stand up for our rights!

Father (*joins in conversation*): But war is so foolish. It brings nothing but trouble to everyone.

Fourth Traveler: There are times when you have to fight for what you believe is right. I read some wise words by Ben Franklin. He said, "Those who would give up essential liberty, to purchase a little temporary safety, deserve neither liberty nor safety."

Stranger (*walking into the inn*): Here, here!

Father (*temper rising*): Whose liberty is at stake? We're arguing over a few pence in taxes — that's all!

Stranger: You want the British telling you what to do? Lobsterbacks patrolling the streets of Boston?

Father: You're referring to the King's army?

Stranger: Lobsterbacks they are! And the only good Lobsterback is a dead Lobsterback. As for King George, he's nothing but a great hairy fool!

Father: That's subversion, sir. And we don't permit subversion here.

Stranger: I thought I was among free men, not slaveys!

Father: There'll be no more talk from you.

(*He pushes the stranger through the door and into the street. Stranger's shouts can be heard off-stage.*)

Mother: Oh, these times! What is going to happen?

Curtain

ACT IV

(Timmy is seated on stool, rest of stage is dark.)

Tim: The summer passed and we still didn't hear any news of Sam. September came, and I went back to school. The leaves turned red and brown in October, and the geese flew south, and the sky turned gray as we turned into November. Then one day Betsy stopped by the inn, as she often did. She asked me if I was going to school this term. It was a dumb question, as she knew I was. "Yes," I answered, and looked at her. She was nodding her head slowly up and down. Sam was back!

I was so excited I could hardly stand it. I felt all sparkly inside — sort of scared and happy both at the same time. The big question was how to find an excuse to get away, so I could see Sam. After lunch, Dad sent me to the woodlot to chop wood. I was trying to figure how to sneak off to see Sam when I first heard the horses. Militiamen had pulled up at the inn. An officer and two men dismounted and went inside. I dropped my ax and hurried back to see what was going on. And what I saw sure scared me.

Light fades on Tim as stage lights go up on main room of inn. Two of the soldiers have Father's arms pinned behind him.)

Officer: We know you have a weapon, Meeker. Where is it?

Father: I don't have it anymore. My son Sam stole it so he could go play soldier boy.

Officer: Come now! You don't expect us to believe that, do you? You're all Tories here. We know that. Where's your gun? *(He jabs his sword against Father's stomach.)*

Father: I'm telling the truth. My son stole it.

71

Officer: But you're a Tory.

Father: That doesn't make my son a Tory, does it? What do you intend to do? Run me through? Make a widow of my wife and orphans of my children?

Officer: I will if you don't surrender your weapon.

Father: Look for yourself. Do you see any gun around here?

Officer: We know you have one. We know where all the Tory weapons are in this town. We need guns. And we're not going to let any Tory keep a gun that could kill a Patriot.

Father: Rebel, you mean.

Officer: Watch you tongue!

Father: But I'm telling you the truth! My son stole the gun so he could join your army. The only weapons here are butcher knives.

Officer: I don't believe you! *(He raises his sword.)*

(Curtain. Spotlight on Tim, seated on stool.)

Tim: At that point I really got scared. I knew those rebels weren't fooling around. They knew Father was a Tory, and they'd kill him, if they had to. After all, he was the enemy.
  I *had* to get Sam. Sam would have the Brown Bess. He could show the militiamen that Father was telling the truth. I ran as fast as I could to where Betsy had said Sam was hiding. He was asleep when I got there. So then I got another idea. Maybe I could take the gun back myself ... *(Tim sneaks up on Sam, grabs the gun, jumps back. Sam awakens, jumps to his feet.)*

Sam: Timmy! What do you think you're doing? Give me that gun before you hurt yourself.

Tim: Don't come any closer or I'll shoot!

(**Sam:** Timmy, don't be crazy!

Tim: Listen, Sam. They're down there and they're going to kill Father if he doesn't give them the Brown Bess.

Sam: Who's down where?

Tim: Militiamen. At the house.

(*Sam lunges for the gun, and wrenches the gun away from Tim.*)

Sam: You little pig! You'd have shot me!

Tim: You're no help! By this time they've probably killed Father!

Sam: I can't go down there. I'm not even supposed to be here.

Tim: You mean you've deserted?

Sam: No, I just thought I'd take off a few days. Men are always sneaking off home for a few days. A lot of the time, the officers don't know where half their men are. If they come around looking for you, your friends lie for you. Still, it's a kind of desertion, and they could hang me for it.

Tim: If you don't help, who will? You want them to kill Father for a gun you stole?

Sam (*thinks a few moments*): All right. I'll come — but just as far as the barn. Just to make sure things are all right. (*Curtain.*)

(Scene: the inn. Mother is applying a bandage to Father's face, when Tim enters.)

Tim: *(Looks around, then beckons to Sam outside):* It's all right. They've gone. *(Sam enters. Father jumps up.)*

Father: You!

Mother: Sam! Where've you been? Are you all right?

Father: Is *he* all right? *(To Sam.)* Your good friends wanted to kill me because of you!

Sam: They didn't know you were my father. As far as they're concerned, you're just another Tory — and they need guns.

Father: Yes. Like the one you stole.

Sam: You don't steal things that rightfully belong to you. This gun is not just your gun. It's a family gun. It gets passed along from father to son, and it would have been mine, anyway. It's my birthright.

Father: When the time comes.

Sam: That time has come. The British won't give us our freedom, so we have to fight for it. We're only taking what is rightfully ours — just as I took this gun. It's a birthright. And when people refuse to give you your birthright, you have to fight for it!

Father: Brave words, Sam. I just hope ...

Mother: He just hopes you don't get killed fighting for our freedom.

Father: Whatever that fine word means.

Sam: I've got to go. *(Walks to door.)* The time for argument is over. We've got ourselves a real fight now. *(Opens door.)*

Mother: *(She, Father, and Tim go to door)*: Be careful, Sam. *(Sam leaves.)*

Father: Sam! Come back, Sam!

(Curtain. Spotlight on Tim, seated on stool.)

Tim: Sam ran across the barnyard and then over the snowy field, carrying the Brown Bess. We watched him till he got to the stone wall at the edge of our pasture. He jumped onto the wall and stood there, looking back at us. Then suddenly he waved, and jumped over the wall, and disappeared into the woods.

It was to be a long war, and a lot of people got killed on both sides. Sam got killed, and Father, he died on a prisoner-of-war ship. After the war Mother and I sold the inn and moved west, to Wilkes-Barre, Pennsylvania. She couldn't bear to stay here.

I guess wars are never very pleasant, regardless of what you're fighting for. Of course, we won our independence, and I'm sure this nation will have a great history. Looking back, I suppose Sam was right. When people don't give you your freedom, you've got to fight for it. It's a birthright. But I wish there could have been another way — a more peaceful way — to get the same thing.

End.

V. *The Bloody Country*

Introduction

The Bloody Country was published in 1976, and it foreshadows the portrayal of slavery and racism that forms the core of the Arabus Trilogy published in 1981, 1983, and 1984. The principal theme we develop is the tension between property values and human values. The secondary theme is that of human ecology, the relationship of man to his physical environment. The necessity to maintain a balance of man's short-term and long-term physical needs while maintaining an environment that will serve, both parallels the need to maintain a balance of human and property values that will best fulfill man's psychological and social needs.

These, of course, are universals that can be demonstrated by study of all societies at all times. We write these books to teach *American* history, however. What we deal with in *The Bloody Country* are interstate relations during the Revolutionary Era, especially under the Articles of Confederation. The conditions of federalism during the Confederation Era are developed largely by implication and require rather more than usual explication by teachers. I will return to these three themes as they are developed in the novel, but first let me explain the historical context of the events we recount.

Historical Context

Though our story begins in 1778, the historical taproot reaches back to 1662. In that year the colony of Connecticut, of dubious imperial legitimacy since its settlement in 1635, received a charter from Charles II legitimating its government and defining its boundaries. The boundary was given as running from where

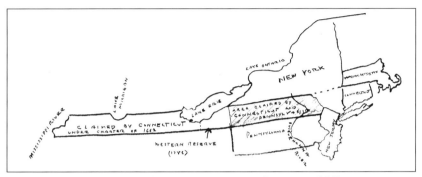

Connecticut Claim Under the Royal Charter of 1662

Narragansett Bay entered the Atlantic Ocean on the south to the Massachusetts line on the north—a distance of about seventy miles—all of the way to the Pacific Ocean—a distance of about three thousand miles. Subsequent grants to the Duke of York (James II) of what became New York and to William Penn of what became Pennsylvania, as the map shows, overlapped these bounds, and indeed cut off Connecticut a few miles east of the Hudson River. By the mid-1700s much of New York's Hudson River Valley had been settled, but the northern third of Pennsylvania that the Connecticut grant overlapped remained pretty much the exclusive domain of Delaware, Shawnee, and other Iroquois-speaking Indians.

The Connecticut colony east of the Hudson flourished economically with agricultural produce not only adequate for its own people but for export as well. The healthy climate, industrious habits, and domestic organization made for large families. Limited space made for population densities insupportable on the thin rocky soil, much of it on rugged ledgy hills. There was not land enough for multiple sons of farmers to have their own farms. Additionally, virtually the whole colony had been cut over to supply wood for building, cooking, and heating. Not only was there a shortage of firewood but because of the disappearance of root systems and summertime shade, hundreds of small streams had dried up or become springtime freshets only. Local water supplies diminished and millstreams vanished.

By the middle of the 18th century large numbers of residents were looking for greener pastures. They trekked to upstate New York, Vermont, and lustfully eyed the fertile well-watered soils of northeastern Pennsylvania. In 1753 a group of enterprising and politically influential speculators in northeastern Connecticut, where the soils and the harvests were thinnest, organized a company to survey and settle the area around the Susquehanna River which was included in the old charter of 1662, Connecticut's basic governing document until 1818. The point of interest was an area running about three miles wide and twenty miles long down the river valley, closed on both sides by hills ranging up to a thousand feet high, known as the Wyoming Valley. (Wyoming is a corruption of a Delaware word meaning "upon the great plain." Its application to the western state is probably due to eastern emigrants.)

Two land companies were formed, the Delaware and the Susquehannah (the terminal h is no longer used). The Delaware Company was ultimately absorbed by the Susquehannah Company. The French and Indian War delayed settlement, but in 1760 Connecticut pioneers went out to the Delaware and in 1762 to the Wyoming Valley. They established farms in a scattered pattern in the area of Mill River with a tiny village at what they soon called Wilkes-Barre. John Wilkes was a member of Parliament who championed the cause of the American colonists and in 1763 was prosecuted for seditious libel after publishing an attack on British government policies. Barre was another parliamentary friend of the colonists.

The area being occupied by the Connecticut settlers was, of course, the home of Indians who, in a fit of resentment at the pioneers' intrusion, massacred them all on October 15, 1763. A royal proclamation of George III of that year established a western limit beyond which colonists were not permitted to venture, but in 1768 the Treaty of Fort Stanwix placed the Wyoming Valley east of the line and thus within the area open to white settlement. Speculators in both Connecticut and Pennsylvania immediately

moved in, went through the motions of buying land from local sachems—or any other Indian they could find—and resold to settlers who then packed up and went off to the Wyoming Valley. Thus in 1769, pioneers began to establish farms under the jurisdiction of both Pennsylvania and Connecticut.

The first forty male settlers from Connecticut built a stockade they called Forty Fort and for a time withstood scattered attacks from the Pennsylvanians, but in late 1769 they were forced out of the valley. Efforts were made by officials in both colonies to have the matter resolved by the King-in-Council—the imperial phase of the conflict. The crown's involvement in the controversy, however, would be ended by American victory at Yorktown in 1781. New bands of pioneers left the area around Windham, Connecticut, in 1771 and were able to establish and reestablish their farms.

In the meantime, efforts by the Connecticut speculators—the Susquehannah Company—to get the colony government to adopt the settlement were successful and the General Assembly created the town of Westmoreland in 1774—about twice the size of the whole mother colony. In 1776 it was made a separate county.

There were about two thousand Connecticut settlers in the Wyoming Valley at that date and about four hundred in Wilkes-Barre village. Militia companies were organized, and other arms of government put in place, including representatives who sat in Connecticut's General Assembly.

When the Revolution broke out in 1775, the Westmoreland militia was withdrawn to fight in the east. Thus at the attack of June and July 1778 by over a thousand enlisted Loyalists, guerrilla Pennsylvania settlers, and Indians, the pioneer families were virtually unprotected. There were about five hundred Indians,

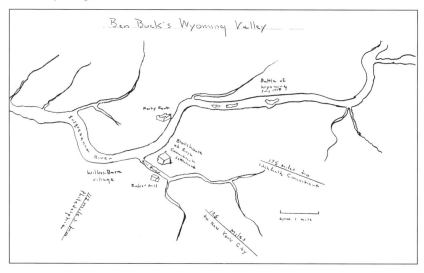

mostly Senecas, described by one historian as "the most ferocious of the Six Nations." The terrified settlers jammed into Forty Fort where Zebulon Butler was able to gather a force of about three hundred men that he foolishly ordered to sally out to meet the enemy on open ground. No quarter was given and Butler's force was nearly obliterated. Despite efforts on the part of English officers to stop them, Indians found and killed many civilians. The massacre at Wyoming Valley was one of the two or three most murderous engagements of the whole Revolutionary War. The British commander counted 227 scalps, and many captives were

FORTY FORT, AS IT IS SAID TO HAVE APPEARED IN 1778.

tortured to lingering deaths. About sixty of Butlers men escaped by fleeing into the hills or swimming across the river. The British claimed they lost only two soldiers and one Indian. Forty Fort and other blockhouses were surrendered, but pillage and murder continued. Hundreds of houses were burned, as well as all the mills, many barns and other buildings. The living remnants fled to the hills and woods where many died; others were taken into captivity by the Indians. "Depopulated and devastated," writes one historian, "the beautiful Wyoming Valley had become a scene of ruin and desolation."

Meanwhile, the Second Continental Congress, which followed the First Congress of 1774, was sitting in Philadelphia trying to supply George Washington and win the war. Both Connecticut and Pennsylvania claimants to the Susquehanna lands petitioned that body to resolve the issue. The Congress took no action until after the Articles of Confederation had been unanimously ratified—an event that finally occurred in March 1781. The Confederation, in Article IX, provided for a mode of settling interstate disputes through the convening of a five-man commission. Pennsylvania immediately set this procedure in motion—the single instance of an interstate judicial proceeding in the entire

Confederation Era. Ultimately, in December 1782, the commission sitting in Trenton, New Jersey, decided every question in favor of the Pennsylvania claimants. Thus the issue of jurisdiction was settled; the Connecticut county of Westmoreland ceased to exist.

Pennsylvania authorities sought to balance the claims of their state's speculators and the few settlers who had bought from them with the claims of the Connecticut pioneers, who by now had well-established farms, mills, churches, and schools. Many Connecticut people accepted alternative lands, and some paid the Pennsylvania speculators. But most saw no justice in either choice. The Pennsylvania claimants sent out Alexander Patterson, whom the government clothed with authority as a justice of the peace, and a company of marshals. Patterson sought to drive the recalcitrant Connecticut people out. This imbroglio led to further deadly confrontations collectively known as the Second Pennamite War.

The last years of the Confederation under the Articles saw a good deal of eleventh-hour desperation on the part of the hard-line Connecticut faction. One John Franklin, who had succeeded the aging and more pliant Zebulon Butler as the most militant leader, tried to launch a movement to establish northern Pennsylvania as a separate new state. He enlisted the aid of one of the young nation's premier land speculators, a man experienced in chipping off new states from old—Ethan Allen of the not-yet-a-state of Vermont. The troubled situation did not need outside agitators. Franklin was hauled off to jail, and Allen made a strategic retreat back to the Green Mountains.

In Congress, meanwhile, Thomas Jefferson chaired a committee that recommended a new commission to try the rights of soil. The Trenton decision had settled only the question of which state had jurisdiction over the area—not which individual claimants actually owned the property. This new trial never came about; rather a political solution was arranged by the Connecticut and Pennsylvania congressmen sitting in Philadelphia. All states claiming territory in the west had ceded their lands to Congress by 1786 except Connecticut. Connecticut still claimed that strip all the way west at least to the Mississippi. The state's delegates in Congress made a deal in which Connecticut would cede that whole claim except for an area—just west of the Pennsylvania line—about the size of Connecticut itself. This territory would be reserved for Connecticut for its use as payment to Revolutionary War veterans and compensation for those Wyoming Valley settlers who would agree to trek to yet another frontier. From those who wouldn't, Connecticut would withdraw political support and leave them at the mercies of the Pennsylvania government. Thus the Connecticut Western Reserve—now the northeast quadrant of Ohio—resolved the property issue for most of the old pioneers and at the same time cleared Congress of its most pressing inter-state controversy just in time to make possible the extraordinary cooperation that characterized the Constitutional Convention of 1787.

Of course, some Connecticut speculators continued to resist the claims of Pennsylvania speculators, and the court system set up under Article III of the new U.S. Constitution and the Judiciary Act of 1789 opened a new field for the contest. The legal question was finally resolved in 1795 in favor of the Pennsylvanians in the well-known Federal case of *Van Horne's Lesse v. Dorrance*. Though the judge determined the legal point, the jury sympathized with Connecticut's Dorrance, awarding the plaintiff seven cents and assessing the defendant for court costs another seven cents.

The sites of action during the Yankee-Pennamite wars are for the most part well known and well marked. The terrible massacre of July 1778 is memorialized by a monument in the borough of Wyoming alongside the Wyoming Avenue, just west of the airport near Eighth Street. Forty Fort was near what is now River Street a little over a mile south of the airport. The Bucks' (fictional) mill was located in Wilkes-Barre on the Mill River just before it forks. This would be in the area of Chestnut Street between River Road

and Main Street across from Hollenback Park where the Wilkes-Barre General Hospital is today. The picture here, taken in June, 1998, shows the site of the Bucks' mill. River Road runs over Mill River and under a decaying railroad trestle, about three hundred yards north of the hospital and one hundred yards east of the shore of the Susquehanna River.

A Note on Emancipation in Pennsylvania and Connecticut

Slavery was legal in Connecticut, and in the 1770s and 1780s there were five or six thousand slaves. Unions of Indian women and black men were common due to a shortage of Indian men. Thus Joe Mountain was not an unusual mixture.

The antislavery movement in Pennsylvania was strong because of the activism there of Quakers. In 1780 the Pennsylvania Assembly enacted a law that required all slave owners to register their slaves; those who were not registered were *ipso facto* emancipated. The law further provided that African-Americans born after 1780 would be free, but must serve their mothers' owners until arriving at age twenty-eight. In general they would have the same rights as indentured servants. In 1784 the Connecticut General Assembly passed a gradual emancipation law that provided that all African-Americans born after March 1784 would become free at age twenty-five; this was soon lowered to twenty-one. But as late as 1848, when slavery was legally ended in Connecticut, there were still a half-dozen elderly slaves in the state.

The Characters

We have borrowed surnames liberally from among the known Connecticut pioneers to the Wyoming Valley, but the combinations with first names are of our own invention. There were plenty of Bucks, but I do not know that any of them ran a mill. We use the name buck to symbolize property. To my surprise, I find that in the late 1990s many young teen-agers don't know that buck is slang for dollar. Some teachers may have to explain that. There was an African-American in Connecticut in this era named Joe Mountain; he came to a bad end (hung for rape), and bears no resemblance to our character. For us, the name Mountain is supposed to suggest largeness of spirit.

Alexander Patterson is a real figure. He seems to have been pretty much the unscrupulous land speculator we make him out to be. He was clothed with an official appointment by the Pennsylvania Assembly and given a company of Rangers for support. But the Assembly did not wholly trust him—with, it turns out, good reason—and sent out William Montgomery and other officials to oversee him. Patterson was acting pretty much as a freelance; many of his actions, like taking settlers' personal property and evicting them without proper procedures, were illegal. The Pennsylvania Assembly finally abandoned him, and he spent some time in jail. Ultimately, however, he emerged as a wealthy and powerful figure in Pennsylvania.

The Themes
A Preliminary Note on Racism

An underlying element of the scene we set and the story we tell in *The Bloody Country*, as in all of our books about the Revolutionary period, is the pervasive and profound racism of the era. By the time readers get to page 3 they have been exposed to the "Indian equals savage" mentality of western pioneers, and to the African-American as "nigger slave." There is a bit of the conventional sexism of the times thrown in, as well. The irony of white Americans fighting a war for independence while holding more than half a million black Americans in slavery is apparent. Father, however, is not given to ideological statements about freedom and self-government. Instead, he construes independence in strictly economic terms: the ownership of real estate, the ability to choose your own trade, to build an estate to bequeath.

Father accepts black slavery and voices the conventional view of the times that blacks were not like whites—not as smart, not as moral. Slavery even under the kindliest master, one who treats a slave as a member of his family, is still slavery. And American slavery was built on a racist foundation. "I like Joe Mountain," Father tells Ben, "and I've treated him as good as I've treated you. He's a human being even if he is a nigger, and I would never treat him hard. But he's got his place and he's got to keep it." (p. 98)

Joe Mountain both personifies and articulates the slaves' natural urge to be free. Ben is ambivalent about Joe's status throughout, almost to the very end. But as the story ends, his association with Joe—his best friend—had rid him of his racist leanings. Right from the start, we see Ben's ambivalence. Even as a nine-year-old, he muses that since Joe was half Mohegan, he ought to be half free, at least: "...maybe he could be a slave in the mornings and free in the afternoons." (p. 5)

As he grows older, Ben's ideas about race and slavery become more complex. "...Being a nigger or an Indian was supposed to make you different," he says some years later, "but I knew it wasn't so." (p. 49) He is much embarrassed about his father's utter obliviousness to racial sensitivities. At one point Father, in an outburst of unconscious but outrageous irony, refuses to let the family return to Connecticut as agricultural laborers. "No, we're staying," he commands his family, which includes Joe Mountain. "Otherwise we might just as well turn ourselves into nigger slaves." "I didn't say anything," says Ben. "I didn't look at Joe Mountain, either." (p. 61) But in the end, Ben has resolved his uncertainties. He is not only reconciled to Joe's freedom, but thinks it is the right outcome:

> But I never forgot him, either, and especially I never forgot the night of the flood, when we sat up in the high meadow and I tried to talk him into coming back to be our nigger. For years afterward I thought about that: and I guess the only lesson I found in it is that it's hard as hell to spend your life never belonging to yourself. No one wants to be a slave, whether it's the kind Joe Mountain was with a master who owned him, or the kind I almost got to be—having to work for somebody else with no chance of building something for myself. Most people are no different from Joe Mountain or me: they can't stand being slaves, and they'll do anything to get out of it. They'll even take a chance of getting themselves killed for it. And the other thing I figured about that is, it doesn't much matter whether you're white or black or Indian or a mixture, the way Joe Mountain was; to be a slave feels about the same for everybody. (p. 181)

Property and Freedom

The central theme that we try to articulate throughout *The Bloody Country* is that human happiness seems to depend on a balance of human—or perhaps humane—values and property values. The human value we emphasize in this novel is the need to command one's own destiny—capsulized in the word freedom. Associated with it are such elements of life as marriage and family, the choice of occupation, and the ability to move around. Property values are in some ways more basic because they include the possession of adequate food, clothing, and shelter. But they also include the right to possess capital goods—if only an ax—necessary to acquire the basics. Beyond that, property values involve governmental protection of property, and the right to enjoy the fruits of one's own labor. Note the conflict between these two that is inherent in the institution of chattel slavery. Note also that the right to the rewards of one's own labor is an element of both freedom and property. Property rights also include the right of bequest and inheritance and the enjoyment of material goods, both real and personal—let us say, houses and wagons, for instance, or mills and slaves. Thus, says Father about Joe Mountain, "He's property, Ben. I ground Colonel Dyer's corn for years and never got a penny—just a little three-year-old sambo. ... He's an investment, Ben, like the millstones." (p. 102)

Father understands the relationship between property and independence. "If you don't own your own land," he declares, "you can't be your own man." (p. 16) On another occasion he insists, "I won't spend my life doing day labor for another man ... I don't want to live half a man." (p. 46) When finally confronted with the human costs of holding on to his property—the deaths of his wife and son-in-law so far, and at the looming risk of the rest of his family—he still refuses to leave the mill. "What kind of a man are you to risk your family just to save your precious mill?" cries his daughter, widowed by her husband's efforts to protect the mill. "I am running this family, and you will do as I say," is his hard-hearted response (p. 133).

At this point, however, unlike Father, Ben's commitment to the mill is only *intellectually* articulated. It is *emotionally* established, however, at the point where he challenges neighbors who are cutting trees along the riverbank. The deforested bank will ultimately ruin the stream as a power source just as overcutting had driven the Buck family from their mill site back east. Ben braves the wrath of woodcutters and takes a beating for it. The painful episode awakens his awareness of the power of property. "... if I could get myself into a fight over a few trees getting cut down," he muses, "was it surprising that men would have a war over a whole valley?" (p. 84) There was a mill on Mill Creek at the site we have located our fictional one, but no picture of it exists. It would have looked very much like this one.

In the early phases of our story, then, Ben was less committed to property than his father. He is, after all, too young to be concerned about his future material welfare, and takes for granted what the family has. His engagement with real estate is fostered when he begins rebuilding his father's mill: "... I worked on the mill a lot by myself. The truth was, it was more my mill than it was his." (p. 144) By the time the mill was completed, Ben had become thoroughly committed to this piece of property. "Now I knew it was time to leave the valley and suddenly I didn't want to go. ... I guess a lot of it had to do with the new mill. I'd built it myself. ... I wasn't just somebody's son, I was a real miller. I could do something most people couldn't do. And I didn't want to give it all up and go back to Connecticut and work on Uncle John's farm for the rest of my life." (pp. 151-52)

Ben's concern with property is set as a counterpoint to Joe's concern for his own freedom. Ben's increasing ambivalence about Joe's slave status reflects his growing understanding of what it's like to be in someone else's thrall. At first he can't see why Joe would want to leave the mill; after all, the two boys had been treated just the same ever since Joe joined the family when both boys were three years old. But as Ben realizes that he, too, would be without a life of his own unless he could hang on to the mill, he begins to understand Joe's longing to be free. Very early in our story, Ben speaks of his father's view that without the mill, "I wouldn't be any better off than Joe Mountain." (p. 47)

Joe, for his part, gets jolted into a recognition of his status in the family when Father dismisses the idea of going back to work on his bother John's farm with the comment, as we've seen, that "we might just as well turn ourselves into nigger slaves." (p. 61) Only a few days later Joe learns that a new Pennsylvania statute has technically emancipated him. He now begins to think seriously about running away (p. 67-68). Ben struggles with his own emotions: Joe has been his playmate and best friend all his life—"just like we were brothers ... I didn't want to suddenly start bossing him around or making him do jobs for me. But still, I wanted to be the white man and him to be the nigger. That was the way it always had been." (p. 68)

Joe leads Ben along to some comprehension of what it means

to be a slave. "Suppose Father freed you, what different would it make?" Ben asks. "It wouldn't change anything." Joe replies, "I wouldn't have to stay here. I could travel around, and choose different kinds of work. You'll stay because you'll get the mill. But a slave can never own anything." (p. 91) This conversation shakes Ben up enough so that he gives Joe's status a lot of thought. "A few times I tried to sort of close my eyes and see what it felt like to be a slave. Suppose it was me instead of him? Suppose all I had to look forward to all my life was working at the mill for Father, and then somebody else when Father died, and never get married and have a family ... what would I feel about it then?" (p. 92) And then Ben understands "... if we went back to Connecticut, that's the way it was going to be." (p. 93) "The thing I couldn't get out of my head was, if we didn't want to be slaves to Uncle John, why would Joe Mountain want to be a slave to us." (p. 98)

Joe finally determines to run away and Ben remonstrates with him. "God damn it, Ben, you try being somebody's nigger for a while and see how you like it." (p. 123) Ben tries physically to restrain Joe, but Joe leaves, and Ben walks back to the dispossessed family's temporary camp in the woods. "And all the way back to the camp I kept telling myself that Joe Mountain was wrong, that he shouldn't run off, but should stay with us. But no matter what reasons I told myself in my head, someplace else inside me I knew that I was wrong, and that I'd wrecked it with my best friend." (p. 124) At the end, when it looks like they've lost the mill and there is no hope for the Bucks in Pennsylvania, and indeed Ben is on his way back to Connecticut to work on his uncle's farm, he encounters Joe. In the thematic climax of the book, Ben thinks, "All of a sudden I realized something queer. Now it was Joe who was going to grow up free and be his own man; and it was me who was going to be somebody's slave." (p 176)

Ecology

Racism, property, slavery make up the central theme of our story. But a very strong secondary theme—one of even greater interest now at the turn of the century than when we wrote *The Bloody Country* in the mid-1970s—is that of human ecology. Ecology is the study of the relationship of organisms to their environment. Here we are concerned with natural water power and the effect of deforestation.

By the late 18th century most of Connecticut's five thousand square miles had been denuded of the great primeval forests of hemlock, pine, fir, oak, hickory, chestnut, elm, and other conifer and deciduous trees that had once been home to Indians and their animal prey. An average family of Connecticut colonials needed fifteen to thirty cords of wood every year. (A cord is a pile four feet high and wide and eight feet long.) As early as the 1790s some urban centers like New Haven were importing fire wood, not only from inland areas but also by boat from places as far away as Maine. Indeed, local ordinances against cutting in the common town woods were passed in some communities as early as the late 17th century. Farmers were driven to building stone walls rather than rail fences of chestnut and cedar. As the woods were clear-cut to make way for meadows, pasture, orchards, and arable acres, and to supply the heating, cooking, and building needs of the English settlers, the shadeless fields dried out. Without the dead leaves that covered the ground and absorbed the water and the roots that held the soil, hundreds—probably thousands—of small streams dried up in the summer or disappeared entirely. Scores of small local grist, saw, and fulling mills were left without water to turn their wheels to grind corn, saw planks, and clean wool. This is what happened to the Bucks' mill.

The ecological theme is introduced when Ben rhapsodizes about the lush growth and rich soils of the Wyoming Valley and concludes, "Coming from Connecticut where the trees were practically all gone and the soil was worn out ... it was like coming to

Heaven." (p. 15) In Connecticut "we had to travel nearly a mile to cut wood for the fireplaces ..." (p. 16) Farmers were already moving west for that reason. But the Bucks' big problem was the disappearance of the stream that powered the mill. "As long as there were woods along the streams," Ben explains, "the rain would kind of soak slowly into the ground and seep into the streams and creeks gradually, so they'd run pretty steady all year round. But when the farmers began cutting off the woods along the creek banks the rain water would rush into the creeks full force, and race away down to the ocean, tearing up the banks as they went. Then the creeks would dry up until the next rain." (p. 17) Ben again described this process when he sees it being repeated in Pennsylvania (p. 51), and Father makes the point more emphatically (pp. 77-79). But now it is portentous. Father's concern foreshadows the great flood of 1784. Father tries to persuade other settlers to leave the trees on the riverbank, but to no avail. He points to Connecticut ordinances about such cutting, but his antagonists point out, "That's Connecticut law. That doesn't apply here anymore" [now that the court had given the Valley to Pennsylvania], (pp. 76-77).

In a scene that both forewarns of the coming catastrophic flood and provides Ben with the last necessary experience to understand the power of the property urge, Ben gets beaten up trying to stop the ecological depredation of woodsmen desperate to feed their families (pp. 82-84). The trees along the banks of the river are cut, and that condition contributes to the flood that washed away the Bucks' mill and most of the rest of Wilkes-Barre. The flood was pretty much as we describe it—perhaps worse (pp. 129-31). Indeed, these flood conditions had just been repeated in 1975, a year before *The Bloody Country* was published, and residents of Wilkes-Barre told us of events and conditions even more frightening and costly in human and material terms that those of 1784.

The lack of ecological foresight and discipline brought havoc to the village. Pioneers who had built in the river bottom—along the flood plain—lost their houses and barns, and often a good deal of soil as well. Some even lost acres where the river course had moved and put their fields within someone else's property lines. That was a lesson not learned: Much of the property damage of the flood in 1975 occurred in the same place—on the flood plain.

The Bloody Country: Chronology

The Bloody Country: Bibliography

The principal source of information on the Yankee-Pennamite Wars is an eleven-volume scholarly edition of *The Susquehannah Company Papers* edited by Julian P. Boyd and Robert J. Taylor, published between 1936 and 1971 by the Wyoming Historical Society. Whether the colony government should sponsor the Susquehannah Company's claims dominated Connecticut politics from 1769 to 1774. This story is the subject of a 1972 University of Connecticut doctoral dissertation by Richard Thomas Warfle, "Connecticut's Critical Period: The Response to the Susquehannah Affair, 1769-1774." Other important works are:

Boyd, Julian. *The Susquehannah Company: Connecticut's Experiment in Expansion.* New Haven, Conn.: Connecticut Tercentenary Commission, 1935.

Brady, James Edward. "Wyoming: A Study of John Franklin and the Connecticut Settlement in Pennsylvania." Unpublished Dissertation, Syracuse University, 1973.

Cooke, Jacob E. *Tench Coxe and the Early Republic.* Chapel Hill: University of North Carolina Press, 1979.

Harvey, Oscar Jewel. *History of Wilkes-Barre.* 6 vols. Wilkes-Barre, Pa.: Readers Press, 1909-30. 6 vols.

Matthews, Alfred. *Ohio and Her Western Reserve.* New York: D. Appleton and Company, 1902.

Taylor, Robert J. "Trial at Trenton." *William and Mary Quarterly.* 3rd Series. 26 (October 1969) 4:502-47.

Warfle, Richard T. *Connecticut's Western Colony: The Susquehannah Affair.* Hartford, Conn.: American Revolution Bicentennial Commission of Connecticut, 1979.

Williamson, James R. "Connecticut's Bloodiest Battle of the Revolution." *Bulletin* of the Connecticut Historical Society. 46 (July 1981) 3:86-96.

_____. "A Connecticut Settlement in Northeastern Pennsylvania: The Yankee-Pennamite Wars." *Bulletin* of the Connecticut Historical Society. 45 (January 1980) 1:22-32.

VI. *The Winter Hero*

Historical Context

Pelham, Massachusetts, was settled in 1740 by a group of Scotch-Irish Presbyterians who fled the wrath of the Congregational town fathers in Worcester about forty miles to the east. Boston is another forty; and the New York line is a little over fifty miles west as the crow flies.

In 1786 Pelham was a fairly typical farm community of about a thousand people spread over roughly thirty-two square miles of rocky hills. Today it is a small dot just east of Amherst on Route 202. Daniel Shays' house and the Conkey Tavern were located in a section called East Hill that was divided off as the town of

THE OLD CONKEY TAVERN

HOME OF CAPTAIN SHAYS

Prescott in 1822. Ironically, or perhaps appropriately, the town was named after Dr. Oliver Prescott, who was active on the government side during the insurrection. Between 1937 and 1946 much of the area was flooded to make the Quaban Reservoir. Most of Prescott was submerged; what is left is now within the bounds of New Salem. A strip of land about ten miles long called Prescott Peninsula, open to the public only by permit, is a state wildlife preserve. Daniel Shays' house was there and a cellar hole is still visible. The exact location of Conkey's Tavern is debated locally: Some say a cellar hole is still visible, others insist that the site is under water; but all agree that it is on the Prescott Peninsula.

These pictures of the Conkey Tavern and Daniel Shays' house were taken in the very late 19th century. They were used to illustrate C.O. Parmanter's *History of Pelham*, published in 1898.

In 1786 there were about two hundred men of fighting age in Pelham—one historian says 217—and ninety of them took up arms against the government during the insurrection. These were small farmers, on the edge of self-sufficiency, only a few of whom had actually mortgaged their farms. But they all had friends or relations who faced debtor's prison, and two or three were already there. Why?

The fiscal history of the Confederation period is terribly complex and has been analyzed and explained by a number of scholars whose works appear in the bibliography below. I will try to simplify without introducing inaccuracy. During the Revolution, the Continental Congress had printed paper money and issued notes, that is, IOUs to be paid with interest at some future date, backed up by nothing more substantial than its ability to borrow gold and silver coin—specie—from France, Dutch bankers, and those Americans willing and able to lend specie. These "Continentals" of 1776 promised an exchange for gold or silver, but Congress had none to give. The state governments also printed paper money and issued notes. The state governments, unlike Congress, had the power to tax their citizens and lay duties on imports collectable at their ports. The effort was to collect enough hard currency to pay the interest on the loans certainly, and the principal if possible. In many instances citizens could use the paper notes to pay taxes. Governments hoped that by reducing the amount of paper in circulation, the value of it would stay close to its face value—par. The Congress called on the states to make contributions—requisitions—in both specie and U.S. notes, but very little specie found its way there.

The result of all this was that the paper money of both the states and Congress depreciated very rapidly and very deeply. Paper money issued by the Continental Congress was officially valued at one specie dollar to forty paper dollars by the end of the war. Actually, however, paper currency and notes circulated at much less than that, some state and U.S. notes had sunk to one thousand paper dollars for specie valued at one dollar. A very significant portion of these notes had been bought up by speculators. These speculators constituted a highly influential lobby for redemption in both Congress and the state legislatures. Thus in Massachusetts, the General Assembly in the spring of 1786 enacted the largest specie tax that it had ever levied. The income, along with state import duties, was to be used to pay interest on the public debt—interest that would go largely to speculators. (We try to explain this on pp. 14-16 of *The Winter Hero*.)

Looking at this situation from the perspective of our middle- class farmers in western Massachusetts, we see a very grim scene. Here are soldiers who have left their farms—in some cases for years at a time—who, for their sacrifice, hold "soldiers' notes" issued by the Congress or the state with a face value of, let us say, six hundred dollars. On returning to their neglected and probably fairly run down farms, they must repair their fortunes. Their notes, they discover, are worth only pennies on the dollar and going down every day. They might hold on to them in hopes that the states—or maybe even Congress—will someday redeem them at par and with interest. But there are too many things needed to bring their farms up to prewar production; axes, hoes, plows, livestock, and the like. These capital goods have to be bought at the local stores where the proprietor will take their notes only at one-quarter, one-tenth, or one-fiftieth of their value. The storekeeper, in turn, will sell the notes to the speculators who made their regular rounds through the countryside.

Now, the Massachusetts General Assembly—dominated by the speculators and other public creditors, some of whom actually sit as voting members—levies a tax that must be paid in specie. Our country farmer has no specie. He borrows from the neighborhood merchant, large property owner, or other local monied man; his livestock, his capital goods, his farm are his collateral. Six months later when the crop is in, he expects to pay it off; but there is not enough wheat or corn or pork to cover. The creditor closes in. And the farmer's creditor, let us say, is also a speculator in paper notes and a representative to the General Assembly who voted to tax our farmer in order to realize a profit on the notes the farmer had received for his miserable years in the army, but has had to exchange for necessities. Our farmer is outraged. (pp. 14-16, 48-49)

Western Massachusetts, frontier country with dangerous Indians until a generation before the outbreak of the Revolution, had a history of riotous political expression. Patriot mobs shut down the courts of Loyalist judges on the eve of hostilities in 1775. Antitax groups did the same thing in 1783.

Now in 1786 the same forces came into play. Many of the settlements west of the Connecticut River had not been incorporated into towns, and so had no representatives in the General Assembly. Others, for one reason or another, did not send representatives. Since the towns had to pay the expenses and salaries of their representatives, many just thought it was not worth the cost. That cost was a significant matter is demonstrated by contrast with Connecticut, where the state paid the expenses and attendance was always nearly complete. A full representation from the western towns would have mitigated the fiscally oppressive acts, and maybe prevented them entirely as was the case in neighboring states.

Specie taxes and depreciated currency were not the only grievances of the Massachusetts agricultural community during the

Confederation years. Conventions of farmers going back to 1782 had complained of the high costs of court fees assessed against the debtors the lack of representation in many western settlements not incorporated as towns; too many public servants with salaries too high; the sitting of the government at Boston instead of some central place; and too many lawyers. (p. 16) The farmers also called for new issues of paper money; stay laws that would postpone the payment of private debts and public taxes; reform of the system of taxation that weighed heaviest on owners of real estate—typically farmers; and the annual election of all civil officers. Additionally, there were widely believed rumors of an impending coup that would turn the state government over to the military or to wealthy Boston creditors who would cut the state up into "lordships."

None of the grievances were redressed by the General Assembly in 1786; indeed, as I noted earlier, the most burdensome tax of the whole era was levied at this time. Facing the loss of essential possessions like plows and livestock or even barns and pastures, farmers gathered in county conventions in Worcester, Hatfield, and other places. Petitions drawn up and sent to the General Assembly gained no result. The distressed and even desperate farmers organized themselves into companies and surrounded courthouses where foreclosures were threatened. In several places they succeeded in intimidating the judges or physically preventing them from entering the courthouse. In August and September 1786 courthouses were forced to close in places as widely separated as Northampton, on the Connecticut River, and Concord outside of Boston. But the area of most agitated unrest was Hampshire County, west of the Connecticut River. Early meetings were held in nearby Pelham, Daniel Shays' hometown, about fifteen miles east of the river, twenty-five miles north of Springfield. At last, the most energetic and perhaps less disciplined, and certainly the most financially insecure, debtors gave up on peaceful assembly and petition and readied themselves for armed combat.

It is easy to see why Shays wanted to capture the Springfield Arsenal. It consisted of a wooden storehouse, barracks, and workshop; a strongly built brick magazine; and a foundry for casting brass cannon. In 1786 there were 450 tons of military good stored there, including 7,000 muskets with bayonets, 1,300 barrels of powder, and a large supply of shot. It is less easy to understand *how* Shays thought he could take the arsenal. Long before he left Pelham, militia General William Shepard had collected at least six hundred men inside the Arsenal, built a palisade around the buildings, and sent for help from the east. It was widely believed in the aftermath of the battle that much of the initial spirit of the Shaysites was alcoholic. Certainly the decision to attack up an open hill in the face of cannon was not the wisest.

If I might enter a literary note here, I can explain the somewhat artificial element in our story when Justin is assigned to the crew tramping down the crusted snow. In first-person narrations, our storyteller always has to observe the action firsthand; or nearly always. Some secondhand description of events can work, but it is difficult to maintain pace, suspense, and the sense of immediacy that an eyewitness or participant can give. Thus Justin has to be up at the head of the column where he can observe the parlay between Shays and Buffington. (pp. 74-75)

That encounter, incidentally, actually happened pretty much as we have it, even down to the words used by the two commanders. Perhaps I should point out the authenticity of the fact that both Shays and Buffington were dressed in old Continental Army uniforms. This implies that the conflict included elements of *civil war*, though, of course, it was much more like a revolution or insurrection since it was aimed at the government.

The rout of Shays' troops on January 25, 1787, was both the central act and the climax of the rebellion. From there on for the rebels it was run and hide and run again. The successful surprise attack at Petersham up a nearly impassable mountain pass in the midst of a blizzard took place on February 4. The battle at Egremont was on February 27. The total number of casualties is unknown. Several men on both sides froze to death; there were the two boys, Levi Bullock and Tom Mayo, who suffocated in the potato hole; and a couple of General Benjamin Lincoln's men died of pneumonia after the action was over; four Shaysites died at Springfield; and one government artilleryman lost his arms in an accident there; an aide to Shays was killed by his own men by mistake; four rebels died in battle at Sheffield. With the reports using quantitative vagaries like "some" and "several," it is impossible to tell how many casualties there were, but I would put the figure at under twenty-five altogether for both sides.

In the elections following the insurrection, however, Shaysites voted in large numbers, filled many chairs in the next Assembly, and began the process of fiscal relief and reform that they had been unable to gain by force of arms.

By then the nation's leading political figures had gathered in Philadelphia (May 1787) to revise the Articles of Confederation, or—as it turned out—replace them with an entirely new Constitution. The delegates were profoundly affected by the insurrection in Massachusetts. For several years many state and national leaders had feared an uprising of the debtor class, and at last it had come. In no small measure were the delegates in Philadelphia moved to strengthen the central government by giving it the power to tax and to act in cases of insurrection because of their perception of events in Massachusetts. When the draft constitution came before the voters in the Massachusetts towns outside the immediate vicinity of Boston, majorites were opposed to adopting it. Indeed, the constitution was nearly rejected in Massachusetts, and only last minute concessions by the Federalists and an eleventh-hour endorsement by Governor John Hancock brought ratification. Because Massachusetts, one of the "Big Three" states was essential to the success of the new government, the Shaysites came close to aborting the Union.

The story as we tell it follows exactly the historical chronology. The dates we give for events can be relied on as the dates you would find in scholarly accounts. The episodes were fairly easy to reconstruct because the rebellion, by 1977 when we wrote the book, had been fairly well studied by historians. (The most valuable secondary scholarly studies have been published since *The Winter Hero* was written and are listed in the bibliography at the end of this essay). But more useful to us were the very full, very detailed records in the Massachusetts Archives. Here are all the relevant records of the General Assembly and the Governor's Council, along with the originals of military reports, petitions for relief before the insurrection and clemency after it.

In particular, I might note that the abortive attack on the Springfield Arsenal, the flight to Petersham, the raid there, and further flight and skirmishes like that at Egremont follow the historical record as exactly as we could make them. The death of Bullock and Mayo in the potato hole are especially poignant realities.

The story of the escape of McColloch and his jailmates with the help of their wives is authentic. Historically, the prisoners involved were Peter Wilcox and Nathaniel Austin, who had been captured during the engagement at Egremont. The men became friends while confined in the Great Barrington jail. Austin was twenty-two years old and had three little children. Wilcox was a laborer, "unskilled in the true principles of government. . . wholly ignorant of the Rights of the Constitution . . . ," according to his petition for clemency, and the father of two "babes." Their wives did get Abel Holman drunk and then switched clothes with their husbands. The sixteen-year old Holman himself was jailed for permitting the escape. It is their wives' petition beginning "Lett not? Oh Lett Not?" that we quote (p. 143). Indeed all the italicized material is verbatim from the records kept in the Massachusetts Archives.

The many discussions in the council presided over first by Governor James Bowdoin and then Governor John Hancock as to the disposition of the insurrectionists are reported in the archives materials. Here one can follow the suspenseful series of sentencings and reprieves. We give the impression that the reprieve of

June 22 was a final one, but in fact it was only another delay—to August 2, when yet another reprieve came forth. The unconditional pardon was granted by Hancock and the council on September 20. The scene we describe with the men standing on the scaffold with the rough knotted rope chaffing their necks took place on June 22. The scene as we describe it is exactly as reported in formal and informal accounts. Two ministers, Enoch Hale and Moses Baldwin, preached at the hanging—one of them (my sources differ) from Romans 6:21. "What fruit had yee then in those things, whereof ye are now ashamed? for the end of those things is death."

Chronology

The first time we provide readers with a specific date is on page 49, and then we only know that the action is taking place some time between October 1786 and January 1, 1787. Below I give the dates for specific events portrayed or alluded to in our story.

Extralegal conventions of antigovernment forces met on town and county-wide bases all through the late summer and fall of 1786. A large convention for Hampshire County was held at Hatfield on August 22. The courthouse at Northfield was taken possession of in late August by about fifteen hundred men. On August 31 there was a mass meeting on Pelham Hill. Courts were closed by mob pressure in several places in September. Shays began to enlist troops on October 23, 1786. A special session of the General Assembly convened and it suspended the right to a writ of habeas corpus, but made some concessions to the conventions' petitions, and gave the mobsmen until January 1, 1787, to renew their oaths to the government.

Shays and other leaders brought men to close the court at Springfield on December 26. Governor Bowdoin issued an order for the arrest of Shays and sixteen other leaders for treason on January 10, 1787, and a sheriff was sent out to capture them.

Government troops under Benjamin Lincoln began to assemble in eastern Massachusetts on January 18 and reached Worcester on January 22. Shepard gathered six hundred men at Springfield on January 24. The attack on the arsenal took place on January 25. Shaysites fled; Shays to Chicopee on January 27. Lincoln with two thousand men arrived in Springfield also on the 27th. Immediately he pursued various contingents of Shaysites fleeing in different directions.

Shays remained under siege at Pelham until February 3 when he and the bulk of his forces retreated north, but were attacked at Petersham with many taken prisoner on February 4. Wholesale surrenders of Shaysites took place over the next ten days. Hungry, frustrated remnants of disorganized rebels pillaged Stockbridge February 27. This was the same day as the engagements at Sheffield and Egremont. The two boy rebels suffocated at Lanesborough on March 3. McColloch's trial was at Great Barrington, April 8; the jailbreak on about June 10. The gallows' episode took place on June 22, 1787.

The Characters

There were lots of Conkeys in Pelham, but we made up the family that is central to our story. It is enough, perhaps, to say that our Justin is fourteen in 1786. Peter McColloch is based on one Henry McColloch who was captured and sentenced to die. (A frequent variant spelling is McCulloch.) In petitions for clemency submitted by McColloch, his mother, and some local dignitaries like Major Mattoon, McColloch is described as "a high fellow," rash and imprudent in his language, but who will be a good citizen if spared. On his own behalf, McColloch wrote that he was pushed to the fore because he had a good horse and "a foolish fondness to be thought active and alert." He claimed he had left home unarmed but was persuaded to take an old cutlass for show just before the attack on the arsenal.

Billy Conkey, whom we have as Justin's uncle, was in fact William Conkey, a taverner in Pelham, just down the main road to Springfield from Shays, "in the Hollow." He was known locally as Billy, and had served a couple of terms as Pelham town clerk. In 1787 was thirty-five years old.

OLD CONKEY TAVERN SIGN. (FRONT AND BACK)

Daniel Shays, of course, was also a true historical figure. Shays was thirty-nine years old in 1786. He grew up poor, but after the war he bought a farm on Pelham East Hill, in what later became the town of Prescott. In 1775 he answered the Lexington Alarm and was with the forces at Bunker (Breed's) Hill. He went on the expedition that took Fort Ticonderoga under Ethan Allen's leadership, served with Varnum's Rhode Island regiment, and with "Mad" Anthony Wayne. Shays was at Burgoyne's surrender at Saratoga and at the victory at Stony Point on the Hudson. He was mustered out with Rufus Putnam's regiment in 1780. He was, in fact, given a sword by Lafayette and did, in fact, sell it to pay his debts. For this he was never forgiven by his fellow officers, who looked down on him anyway as uncouth.

Shays left Pelham owing money—some to his friend Bill Conkey, and ultimately his property was taken for taxes. After the insurrection he remained in Vermont until 1791, though he was granted a pardon by the Commonwealth of Massachusetts in 1788. He moved from Vermont to Sparta, New York and died there in 1825, age seventy-eight. He is buried in the Union Cemetery at Conesus, New York. We have Justin refer to Shays as General; subsequent to publishing *The Winter Hero* I learned that Shays was called General only by government forces as a taunting sarcasm.

Ebenezer Mattoon, a militia captain during the Revolution, was by 1786 a major, a justice of the peace and a leader in church and society in Amherst, the next town west of Pelham. He was a large landowner, farming some acres himself and renting out others. Mattoon was immensely unpopular, and claimed he "suffered much in person and property" at the hands of the rebels. As the uprising raged, he was forced with his family to seek refuge in a neighboring town. Nevertheless, after the insurrection, he petitioned on behalf of McColloch arguing that "if he is spared the town of Pelham is attached to government; if he is executed . . . the affections of the town is lost." By the time of the War of 1812, Mattoon was a militia general.

Other historical figures include the generals William Shepard, Benjamin Lincoln, and Rufus Putnam. Theodore Sedgewick, Sheriff Porter, Samuel Buffington, and Royal Tyler are also real and did as we have them do in the story.

Literary Analysis: The Themes
Introduction

The Winter Hero, like *The Bloody Country*, is set during the years of the United States' first constitution, the Articles of Confederation (1781-1789). We try to show the kinds of problems that arose under the Articles: overlapping state territorial claims in *The Bloody Country*, and fiscal chaos and resultant agrarian unrest in *The Winter Hero*. These two books, with *Jump Ship to Freedom*, deal with the years immediately preceding the ratification of the Constitution in 1788. Our effort is to give students some insight into the great advantages Americans have enjoyed under the document written and ratified well over two centuries ago.

In *The Winter Hero* we attempt to make the case, also, that political processes in general can be more effective than physical confrontation. We try to shed some light on the economic basis of political conflict, on the level of both specific grievances and class antagonisms. An underlying theme that is articulated in the book's title is that glory sought for its own sake can be ephemeral at best and probably counterproductive. Let's survey each of these themes in turn.

Political Participation and the Legitimation of Authority

Early on we point out that at least part of the western Massachusetts farmers' economic problems resulted from their failure to exercise their political muscle. We have Daniel Shays explain that the General Court is dominated by lawyers and wealthy merchant creditors. "I thought we could vote in whoever we wanted," Justin asks. "Unfortunately," Shays explains, "a lot of towns in this part of the state didn't send representatives to our legislature. ..." (p. 16) After the collapse of the insurrection Justin has learned "We realized how stupid we'd been. Dozens of towns hadn't bothered to send representatives. . . . We could see now that if we'd had more sense and sent people . . . we would have been able to pass at least some of the laws we wanted. It seemed likely that we'd never have had to fight." (pp. 129-30) In the context of this political material, we take the opportunity to point out that political rights were not universal. Molly would not have been typical in her outrage at being denied the suffrage, but neither would she have been alone (pp. 131-32).

Justin accepts the justification of the insurrection as a matter of onerous taxation, just as it was in 1775, but he looks for a more principled rationale for going to war just as did the Revolutionary leaders in 1776. He explores the question of how authority gains its legitimacy in two conversations: one with his sister, the spunky Molly (pp. 62-63), and one with the sophomoric Levi Bulloch (pp. 90-93).

Molly says that authority—in this case that of her husband—is legitimate when the governors are guided by the welfare of the governed, and in fact work to fulfill those needs. It is significant that Molly does not say that it's her place to *serve* her husband as would have been conventional, but rather to *help* him (p. 63). Molly is modeled on the real McColloch's young wife, who exhibited extraordinary enterprise in not only petitioning the governor but walking to Boston and personally presenting her petition to him. Our Molly sees clearly that the established authorities were either ignorant of the common Massachusetts farmers' conditions in the 1780s or deliberately trying to enrich themselves at the farmers' expense. "Major Mattoon gives orders just to get the best for himself," she explains. "That's wrong. The one who's in charge ought to be looking out for everybody." (p. 64)

The cynical fifteen-year-old Levi Bulloch has a different and very simplistic take on the matter. Justin makes the Lockean case that government is supposed to serve the public. The General Court is "supposed to do what we want *them* to do," Justin declares. "The government is supposed to see that everybody gets a fair shake," (p. 90) says our narrator in a statement echoing the justice suggested in his name. But Levi counters with the statement that it doesn't matter what the governors are supposed to do, ". . . you put a man on top and the next thing you know he figures he's got a right to be on top. . . . They even figure they have a right to own all the property, too." (p. 91)

Levi does not see the insurrection in terms of principles. It is, rather, a simple economic conflict. ". . . when we ask for new laws so we can keep our farms and feed our families, why, they tell us to shut up." (p. 92) Power was purely a matter of economic motivation. "It's human nature for the rich to want to stay rich, and the poor to want to get rich and for the ones on top to push on the ones below, and it's human nature for the ones on the bottom to push back." (p. 93) Justin sees a bit more complexity: It was a matter of both economics and politics. "I just wanted to keep what was mine, and not have anybody lording it over me." (p. 93) However, Levi knows then and Justin learns later that at least part of the problem was political. "If there's enough of us to beat 'em in battle, there sure was enough of us to elect our people to the General Court. We were stupid not to send our representatives." (p. 92) And Justin after the rebellion has failed, admits, "If we'd sent our people to the General Court in the first place, we might never have had to fight." (p. 150) The point we are making, we hope, is clear enough. The price of liberty is more than eternal vigilance; keeping your rights requires some effort, too. Democracy does not work when the people do not play their part.

The Economic Basis of Politics

Much more pervasive in our story are the economic themes. We do not intend to create the impression that people are not motivated by a quest for power (politics) or prestige, or that family connections and all sorts of psychological and ideological concerns are not important motives for human behavior. But one set of motives is economic, and that is what we try to portray in *The Winter Hero*. We introduce this theme at the very outset in the scene where Sheriff Porter (a real figure) tries to take Peter's oxen. Justin reinforces this economic concern when he worries about the cost of buying a new bucksaw blade (pp. 1-3).

We further personify this economic theme when Justin characterizes Peter as profligate. There was a general belief among much of the propertied class in Massachusetts that the farmers had got themselves in debt by promiscuous spending on doodads and trifles. "They run up debts buying gewgaws—fancy pins and silver buttons. . . ," says Major Mattoon (p. 54). And so, indeed, does our Peter wantonly spend ten shillings for silver buttons for Molly (p. 6). For ten shillings in 1786 you could buy two and a half bushels of corn, or twenty-four pounds of butter, or five gallons of molasses, or sixty quarts of milk, or three pounds of tea, or four quarts of gin, or hire a laborer for five days, or a skilled carpenter or blacksmith for three days. You could even use it to pay down your debts.

Once the narrative is infused with these mundane economic matters, we move on to develop the theme of class antagonism. Ironically, Molly, who is ready to join the rebels and shoot someone over material possessions, castigates the creditor class, "They don't care about people at all—only about things." (p. 10) At base, this insurrection is not about ideology and political rights as was more evidentially the case in 1776, but about economics. "Something's got to be done about the taxes," Peter declares, "something's got to be done about these debts everybody has and going to prison. *And* the court fees, *and* the legal fees, and all the rest of it." (pp. 47-48) Legalities like those constitutional issues that informed the rhetoric of the 1770s, were irrelevant. "It may be legal," says Peter about the dispossession of his oxen, "but it's not right." (p. 3)

Peter is talking about economic justice here. We see this point as a central one; the name of our narrator, Justin, is supposed to suggest equal treatment and fair play—justice. We point out the correspondence of money and power when Molly tries to explain the situation to Justin: "It's hard to understand why we have to struggle so, and lose our oxen, and those like Mattoon have all the money and great houses and don't have to dirty their hands . . . They think they're lords and masters of everything. They think they're high and mighty and we're nothing." (p. 10) The class differences are sketched in Justin's description of the separation of the Mattoon family from the servants on the estate. (pp. 26-27) We learn also that the McCollochs and Conkeys are really not at the bottom of the heap when Jasper tells Justin, he's on Mattoon's side "because it's the only side I've got. . . . You got a little property; Mattoon's got a lot. I don't have any at all. Whose going to take care of me if I lose this job?" (p. 44) Here we imply the Jeffersonian conviction that only the farmer possessed of his own birthright would have the economic security to maintain his political independence.

Speaking of Jasper, if I may add a parenthetical literary note, his drunkenness was representative of the servant class at the time, but it plays its part in our story by making possible Justin's escape after being caught in his small—but daring—act of espionage (pp. 42-47).

The idea that only the people who own property, real estate predominantly, should participate in governing society is known as the "stake in society" theory. Mattoon's colleagues profess this idea. "People with little or no property are not to be trusted," says one (p. 54). "You're right," agrees another, "the common people must understand that the men who own the country are the men who should govern it." (p. 55)

Justin encounters the class division in a very immediate way when he goes to work in the Mattoon household. "When I thought about how hard Molly and Peter worked to put a little johnnycake and syrup on the table while Mrs. Mattoon didn't seem to do much more than a little needlework, but got served fancy food each evening, it made me wonder." (p. 27) He, too, perceives his world in economic terms. He doesn't refer to Mattoon and his peers respectfully as his betters or officers of the government, but as "rich men." (e.g., p. 28) We don't know much at all about the historical Levi Bulloch who died in the potato hole, but we have made him cynical beyond his years when he states the class theory most baldly: ". . . people who have power and money don't like people to be rebellious. They like poor people to do what they're told without making a fuss." Justin, on the other hand, despite all he's been through, has not given up his hopes for justice in government. "I don't believe that's so," he answers (p. 90).

Weather

In a book called *The Winter Hero* it is clear from the start that weather conditions will play a major role. Indeed, commentators in 1786 and 1787 claimed that the winter of those years was the coldest and snowiest since 1717, one that only a few could remember, of course (p. 62). We were lucky that the winter was so severe, however, because a lot of people kept diaries recording daily temperatures, inches of snowfall, and strength of winds. I found a Northampton diary that reported weather conditions for every day of the period our story covers. Readers can be sure that if we say that on January 22, 1787, there was three feet of snow on the fields (p. 69) or that on Thursday, February 1, it snowed three inches (p. 95) that's in fact what it did.

From a historical standpoint, what we are trying to do is convey the pervading impact of weather on these rural and agricultural societies. Weather meant everything to farmers, and droughts, unseasonable frosts, and floods could ruin them. From a boy's perspective, the economic consequences of weather are pretty clear but other aspects of weather are no less evident. "It's a funny thing," Justin notes, "but when you imagine war, you always think about it's being in the summer. It's hard to take an interest in it when your fingers and toes are about to freeze off." (p. 69) [Incidentally, students often ask if this kind of writing grows out of our own military experience. It does not; both James and I served in the army during the Korean War, but neither of us ever left the United States.]

The weather theme is carried into a deeper dimension when we use it in other than its meteorological sense. Connecting weather metaphors to other themes, we have Justin anxiously facing his first military action and wondering, "Would I run if someone came after me? I didn't feel much like a hero: my mouth was dry and my innards cold as ice." (p. 7) He characterizes his feeling about the suffocation of his two young friends: "I was cold as death inside." (p. 125) This is a pretty straightforward statement of our metaphoric equation of death and cold. Finally, Justin describes his reaction to the imminent death of Peter on a hot June day, "As warm and humid as it was, I was as cold inside as I had been all winter . ...." (p. 146)

The Hero

As Timmy's maturation in *My Brother Sam Is Dead* led to his understanding of the deeper meaning of war and its effects on the human condition; and Ben Buck's led to his realization of the varied meanings of freedom in *The Bloody Country*, so Justin Conkey grows in his understanding of politics, economics, and human motivation. He realizes at the end that actions taken strictly for individual aggrandizement—wealth, power, or as in his case, fame—are hollow successes at best and unfulfilling in any event. Communal effort for the general welfare is what pays off most often.

We develop this theme through Justin's efforts to prove himself a hero. That motive is what carries him forward through most of our narrative. The theme is introduced early: "The one thing I wanted, more than anything, was to do something glorious and brave. . . ." (p. 8) Justin's determination to get into the action did not stem from a concern for political justice or even the need to preserve the family's livestock. He wanted "to do something brave and glorious." (p. 18)

Justin gains the support of his sister Molly, who says she will put on men's clothes and go herself if her husband, Peter, will not let Justin join the rebellion. "Want to be a hero, do you?" she asks. "I want to do my share," says Justin (p. 64). The central act in this campaign comes when Peter, bested in the argument by his feisty wife consents: "All right, all right, if he wants to see what war is like, let him. Once he gets shot at the first time," Peter hollers prophetically, "there won't be so much talk about standing up for his rights." (p. 67) And from then on, it's all downhill for Justin's heroic aspirations.

As soon as he begins marching, Justin has to contemplate combat, and he had to admit "I scared me pretty good when I thought about it." (p. 69) He would have preferred marching and fighting in the summertime, he allows, when he pictured an encounter "hand-to-hand with my sword against a militiaman with a bayonet, . . . I didn't feel much like a hero." (p. 71) Then in his first real action, along with most of his fellow rebels, he runs: "I'd had my chance to be a hero and instead I'd run. . . . I'd run like the rest, just turned tail like a coward." (pp. 77, 78) Justin's determination intensifies at first, and he makes another attempt to play the hero (p. 82) and has to conceal his cowardice from Peter. "Had enough of war?" Peter asks. "Oh, no. No, no, Peter, I want to stay," he says out loud; but he thinks, "I just couldn't quit until I'd made up for being a coward." (p. 86)

But disillusion begins to set in when in conversation with the ill-fated Levi Bulloch, Justin comes to realize that his motive for enlisting in Shays' forces was not the glorious one of helping the embattled farmers, but rather, "I was thinking about getting to be a hero. I was out for myself." (p. 93). After he sees blood spilled and draws some himself, acts the hero and is praised for it, Justin realizes that his "heroic" act was not performed out of bravery or courage, but from a more basic emotion of familial love. In his own eyes, there was no heroism at all in saving Peter's life: "It was so hard to believe. I'd been a hero at last without even realizing it. It had been almost an accident. I hadn't *meant* to do anything glorious. I'd just done it to save Peter, and now everybody thought I was a hero." (pp. 120-21)

Justin is confused about the nature of heroism. He ruminates about the matter a good deal. He wants to know, for instance, ". . . didn't you have to be fighting for some glorious cause like God or liberty or something to be a hero? I mean, could you be heroic if you were just fighting against unfair taxes that let rich men get the farms of poor men?" Finally, he decides, "Maybe there weren't any heroes, just ordinary people who were cowards sometimes and heroes sometimes and most of the time just ordinary people. . . . Maybe it would be better to forget about the whole hero problem and just go about my business like everybody else." (p. 123)

Crucially, the deaths of his two friends needlessly, senselessly, in no cause whatsoever, provide Justin with his deepest insight into the matter. "But now, with that picture in my mind of those two fellows in the potato hole, it didn't matter very much anymore that I'd been a hero. What difference did it make when my friends were dead? How could I feel good about it?" (p. 127) And that is the way he resolves it: "One thing I learned," Justin concludes, "was that there wasn't much point in going out to be a hero, because you never know how something is going to look to everybody else. You might as well go along and do your best, and not worry about who's the hero and who isn't." (p. 149)

We hope our readers will see the point and read with proper emphasis "*and do your best*," a high enough aspiration for any of us, and as difficult to achieve as bravery on the battlefield.

In 1927 the Brooklyn, N.Y. branch of the New England Society erected a brass plaque commemorating Benjamin Lincoln's victory over Daniel Shays' forces. Sixty years later at the bicentennial of the Petersham battle a group of scholars and others with a decidedly different perspective erected a plywood plaque (which in 1996 rested in the basement of the Petersham Historical Building, much the worse for wear). The two contrasting inscriptions might challenge your students to look into the historical contexts of 1927 and 1987 to find some explanation for the difference.

IN THIS TOWN

ON SUNDAY MORNING, FEBRUARY FOURTH

1787

DANIEL SHAYS

AND ONE HUNDRED AND FIFTY OF HIS FOLLOWERS

IN REBELLION AGAINST THE COMMONWEALTH

WERE SURPRISED AND ROUTED BY

GENERAL BENJAMIN LINCOLN

IN COMMAND OF THE ARMY OF MASSACHUSETTS

AFTER A NIGHT MARCH FROM HADLEY

OF THIRTY MILES THROUGH SNOW

IN COLD BELOW ZERO

THIS VICTORY

FOR THE FORCES OF GOVERNMENT

INFLUENCED THE PHILADELPHIA CONVENTION

WHICH THREE MONTHS LATER

MET AND FORMED

THE CONSTITUTION OF THE UNITED STATES

OBEDIENCE TO LAW IS TRUE LIBERTY

ERECTED BY THE NEW ENGLAND SOCIETY

OF BROOKLYN, NEW YORK

IN THIS TOWN

ON SUNDAY MORNING FEBRUARY FOURTH

1787

CAPTAIN DANIEL SHAYS

AND ONE HUNDRED OF HIS FOLLOWERS

WHO FOUGHT FOR THE COMMON PEOPLE AGAINST

THE ESTABLISHED POWERS WHO TRIED TO

MAKE REAL THE VISION OF JUSTICE AND

EQUALITY EMBODIED IN OUR REVOLUTIONARY

DECLARATION OF INDEPENDENCE WAS SURPRISED

AND ROUTED, WHILE ENJOYING

THE HOSPITALITY OF PETERSHAM, BY

GENERAL BENJAMIN LINCOLN

AND AN ARMY FINANCED BY THE WEALTHY

MERCHANTS OF BOSTON

TRUE LIBERTY AND JUSTICE MAY REQUIRE

RESISTANCE TO LAW

The Winter Hero: Bibliography

Brown, Richard D. "Shays' Rebellion and the Ratification of the Federal Constitution in Massachusetts" in Richard Beeman, et al. eds. *Beyond Confederation: Origins of the Constitution and National Identity.* Chapel Hill: University of North Carolina Press, 1987.

Ferguson, E. James. *The Power of the Purse: A History of American Public Finance, 1776-1790.* Chapel Hill: University of North Carolina Press, 1961.
Gross, Robert, ed. *In Debt to Shays: The Bicentennial of an Agrarian Revolution.* Charlottesville: University Press of Virginia, 1993. This collection of essays is the place to start. On page 324, there is a list of eight novels, two films, several murals, poems, and musical ballads that tell the story of Shays' Rebellion.

Minot, George Richards, *The History of the Insurrection in Massachusetts in the Year 1786. . . .* Boston: 1788.

Nobles, Gregory H. and Herbert L. Zarov, eds. *Selected Papers from the Sylvester Judd Manuscript.* Northampton, Mass.: Forbes Library, 1976.

Parmenter, C.O., *History of Pelham, Mass. from 1738 to 1898 . . .* Amherst, Mass.: Carpenter and Morehouse, 1898.

Starkey, Marion. *A Little Rebellion.* New York: Knopf, 1955.

Szatmary, David P., *Shays' Rebellion: The Making of an Agrarian Insurrection.* Amherst: University of Massachusetts Press, 1980.

Taylor, Robert J., *Western Massachusetts in the Revolution.* Providence, R.I.: Brown University Press, 1954.

Vaughan, Alden, "The 'Horrid and Unnatural Rebellion' of Daniel Shays," *American Heritage.* 27 (June, 1966).

VII. *The Arabus Trilogy*

General Introduction

The Arabus Trilogy did not start out as a trilogy. Indeed, it very nearly did not start out at all. *The Winter Hero* had been a struggle. Resolving historical and literary conflicts and making revisions suggested by our editor extended the time devoted to it and added a lot of unpleasant, grubby rewriting burdened by more than the usual telephone conferences between my brother and me. I swore I'd never do another one of these historical novels. That was 1977.

I balked when James suggested we try again, but he said, "Look, just give it one day's thought." That seemed like little enough to ask, so I set aside a day to think. Halfway through that day, August 12, 1979, I called James: What did he think of speaking in the voice of a black teenager of 1787? He'd give it a try. I made a preliminary outline. Thirteen months later, we had a final draft to send to our new editor. By the time we finished rewrites and revisions in September 1980, I'd put in about 175 hours on the job; my brother had put in more than that.

Our editor, Olga Litowinski at Dell, loved the manuscript, which was ultimately called *Jump Ship to Freedom*. She wanted another one—no, two more. Let's make it a trilogy, she said; but then came the kicker. Make the next book the story that came *before* the completed one, *Jump Ship to Freedom*. And while *Jump Ship* was still in typescript, think up the prequel story and integrate some of the characters into the already completed *Jump Ship*. That was back in October 1980; the manuscript was to go to the copy editor right away. One November 10 I sketched an outline for the new book, the one that became *War Comes to Willy*

Freeman. I introduced Willy into *Jump Ship* as Daniel's aunt. When I got down to working out the chronology and family relationships for Willy Freeman, a couple of months later, it turned out that she could not be his aunt. I changed her to his cousin. I get scores of letters from alert twelve-year-olds asking how come Willy is Dan's aunt in *Jump Ship* and his cousin in *Willy Freeman*? Now you know the answer.

Working out the third volume was much easier, but still full of problems. We were stuck with ages already established in the first two volumes, and, of course we couldn't mess with the chronology of the actual events. The Nosey of *Jump Ship* is Carrie in *Who Is Carrie?*. If you work hard at it, you might be able to figure out what her age must be. But we fudge that because we want her to be ten years old—which according to the sequence of historical events that form the context of our story, she can't be. We just hope readers won't study the matter too closely.

The Black Experience in Revolutionary America

The theme that ties the three books together is the black experience in the Revolutionary Era. Much has been written in both nonfiction and fiction about black life in the antebellum South. From the fanciful *Gone With the Wind* to the grim *Narrative of the Life of Frederick Douglass*, and, of course, *Uncle Tom's Cabin*, we are treated to widely divergent versions of what it was like to be black in the 19th-century American South. What we try to do is show what it might have been like to be black in the North. Slavery, recall, was legal in every colony, and only in 1780 did any state begin the process of emancipation.

The Connecticut General Assembly began to address the issue in various ways during the years of libertarian rhetoric generated by the white-on-white conflict between Englishmen in England and Englishmen in America. The slave trade, including carrying slaves out of Connecticut with intent to sell, was made illegal in

1774 and in 1784 a gradual emancipation act was passed. There were at that moment about six thousand slaves in the state; when slavery was legally ended there in 1848, there were still a half-dozen blacks held in bondage.

At least five thousand African-Americans fought on the American side in the Revolution as enlistees and draftees. Connecticut contributed over three hundred, among them Jordan Freeman, who figures in *War Comes to Willy Freeman* and Jack Arabus, who is in that book and its sequel, *Jump Ship to Freedom*. Military service was an immense hardship in an agrarian economy where the loss of the labor of sons and husbands often meant the ruin of a family's fortunes. Enlistments were encouraged by congressional, state, and town bounties. Voluntary enlistments did not satisfy George Washington's need for troops, and so every state ulimately resorted to the draft.

Under wartime conditions, free blacks were permitted to join militia companies in New England, but unlike white men, were not required to serve. A number found themselves in combat in 1775 and 1776, but Washington, his council of war, members of Congress, and most state legislators disapproved. In 1775 African-Americans were banned from serving with Continental troops. But in time, filling the ranks of state and Continental units had become a major problem, and beginning in 1777 free blacks were permitted to enlist and slaves were accepted in the draft. It was firm policy, however, that slaves could not be soldiers; thus acceptance into the Continental army ipso facto emancipated slaves. More often than not, however, owners emancipated their slaves at the moment of enlistment.

Our focus in the Arabus Trilogy, however, is not on military life. The forgoing discussion provides the context for the story of Jack Arabus, but our story deals with his fictional young son and niece. We have tried to convey something of the powerlessness of African-Americans, free or slave, and the profound frustrations, disappointment, discouragement, and even torment they faced on a daily basis. Each of the stories in the trilogy portrays a different characteristic of this degraded existence. It is best, then, to discuss each book separately.

The Characters

Fictional

Willy Freeman would have been born in 1768: She is thirteen in 1781 (p. 3). She could have had some education, but here we give her none. Her strong character, dangerously self-assertive for a black female child, must have come from her father, obviously a man of considerable courage and integrity. Ma (Lucy Freeman) is also pure fiction. We do not know if Jordan Freeman was married.

Daniel Arabus would have been born in 1774. The name derives from the biblical Daniel, who was imprisoned in a lions' den by King Darius for worshiping the one-and-only God against royal ordinance. Daniel is saved from injury because "God hath sent his Angel, and hath shut the lyons mouthes." (Daniel 6:22) Our Daniel is several times imprisoned or trapped, but always escapes unhurt.

Mum (Betsy Freeman) is wholly made up. We know nothing of Jack Arabus' family.

Big Tom is purely fictional. He patronizes white folks, and thus his name is supposed to suggest "Uncle Tomming." He explains his position on page 33 of *Jump Ship*.

Birdsey Ivers. The actual captain of the *Junius Brutus* was John Brooks, a stepson of Thomas Ivers. He had a son named Birdsey who was lost at sea at a young age. Otherwise there is no connection to any historical figure.

Peter Fatherscreft was made up, but he resembles the real William Few, whom we introduce and is described in the listing of historical characters. It was important that Fatherscreft be a Quaker because Quakers were the strongest antislavery group in the United States in these years. His name is supposed to sound Dutch and invoke a paternal aura.

Horace, entirely fictional, is based on no one, but springs entirely from James' imagination. None of us, of course, has ever known anyone like him.

Carrie is of uncertain age. We know that when Dan first encounters her, he says she looks to be about ten (*Jump Ship*, p. 96). That was 1787. If Dan's judgement was sound, Carrie was born in 1777, so in 1789 when her story takes place, she would be twelve. This presents no problems unless her own guess that her mother is Lucy Freeman is correct. If Jordan Freeman was her father, she could not have been born later than June 1782; if she'd been born before that, Willy would have known of her. Thus Carrie would be only seven at the time of our story. That is hardly likely. This arithmetic might demonstrate that her conclusion that she was Willy's sister was just another of her wistful fantasies.

It might be an interesting project to set students to sleuthing out the birth dates of these fictional characters by casting their ages against known historical events.

Historical Characters

Jordan Freeman was a servant to Colonel William Ledyard, who lived in Groton. Freeman is spoken of as "powerful," and is buried with the other victims of the slaughter at Fort Griswold, listed on the monument shown here, fifteenth name down in the second column from the left. Other than his heroic action on September 6, 1781, this is all I know about him.

Thomas Ivers was real. Here we incorporate him into a real John Brooks, who was in fact the captain of the real *Junius*

Brutus. Brooks' logs, account books, and journals are at the Discovery Museum in Bridgeport, formerly the Museum of Art, Science, and Industry. We say more about Ivers/Brooks in the section "How Much of this Book is True?" at the back of *Jump Ship.*

William Samuel Johnson was a distinguished lawyer, trained in England, and a very influential Connecticut politician. He had an honorary doctorate from Oxford and was usually called Doctor. He was one of the state's first U.S. senators, but when the capital moved from New York to Philadelphia in 1793, Johnson resigned to stay on as president of Columbia College. He lived in Stratford. His son's house (which we describe on page 14 of *Jump Ship*), in which Johnson died, still stands on Main Street there. He owned slaves, and was one of the men serving simultaneously in both Congress and the Convention. The reference to him as "our delegate to Congress" (p. 1) refers, of course, to the old Congress under the Articles of Confederation.

Samuel Fraunces (1722-95) was a taverner in New York City famous for his wines. Fraunces Tavern was, indeed, "the most noted hostelry of colonial New York." In this tavern Washington bade his famed farewell to his officers after the evacuation of British troops in 1783. Fraunces accepted Washington's invitation to become steward at the presidential mansion. Except for a brief hiatus when Fraunces was replaced for extravagance by John Hyde, as we show, he continued with Washington when the government moved to Philadelphia. Fraunces died there in 1795.

The ambiguity about Samuel Fraunces' race reflects the state of knowledge about that question at the time we were writing *Jump Ship* and *Willy.* A number of historians writing in the 1960s said he was African-American, probably because he was called "Black Sam." There seems to be no other basis for that racial characterization, however. His biographer in the *Dictionary of American*

SAMUEL FRAUNCES.
COURTESY OF FRAUNCES TAVERN.

Biography, published in 1937, takes for granted that he was white. While we were writing *Who is Carrie?*, I became a consultant to a Fraunces Tavern exhibition project where research showed definitively that Fraunces was white, and, as a matter of fact, actually turned up what is believed to be a portrait of the man, shown here through the courtesy of the Fraunces Museum in New York City. This has all been reported in the work by Kym Rice in the bibliography listed below.

Tobias Lear was private secretary to George Washington during the years we cover. His diaries and account books were among our most useful sources. They are listed in the bibliography under Decatur.

128

William Few of Georgia was a member of the old Congress and a
delegate to the Constitutional Convention. His father had
been brought up a Quaker, though Few himself was a
Methodist. But Few had spent several years living in a
Quaker settlement. Few was not the man who carried the
crucial compromise message to Philadelphia. That mes-
senger was most likely either Alexander Hamilton or
Manasseh Cutler, who arrived there from New York on
July 12, the day before the Convention voted on the fugitive slave clause.

Washington, Hamilton, and Jefferson are too well known to
require a sketch here. We do not have Jefferson doing
anything he did not do. But Washington and Hamilton,
obviously, never met Daniel Arabus.

FRAUNCES' TAVERN, AS RESTORED BY THE SONS OF THE REVOLUTION

This picture shows Fraunces Tavern, at 54 Pearl Street in New
York City, as it looks today, an approximate reconstruction of the
original of 1719. That structure, built as a private residence, was
bought by Fraunces in 1762. It suffered fire damage in 1832 and

1852 and extensive alterations as well so that its original appearance cannot be known exactly. This is thought to be as close as historical architects can make it.

War Comes to Willy Freeman

Historical Context

War Comes to Willy Freeman is based for the most part on two episodes from the Revolutionary history of Connecticut. The story begins with a British amphibious raid on New London and on Groton across the Thames River (pronounced in Connecticut the way it is spelled). The Battle of Groton was fought on September 6, 1781, when 1,700 men under Benedict Arnold, the turncoat general who had grown up in New London, launched a two-pronged attack on each side of the river. The objective was the rich spoils from privateering expeditions stored in warehouses and ships lining the harbor. A strategic objective—which failed—was to create a diversion to draw off some of Washington's troops then moving south to what would be the deciding battle of Yorktown.

FORT GRISWOLD IN MAY 1998.

Colonel William Ledyard could rouse only about 150 men to defend Fort Griswold, the remains of which are shown here as they appeared in May 1998. Hundreds of Connecticut militiamen refused to come out of the woods above the fort because they perceived Ledyard's cause as hopeless. Eight hundred of Arnold's crack veterans had been sent against the lightly armed and dilapidated bastion. After bravely, but foolishly, rejecting an order to surrender, Ledyard's men were overwhelmed. The episode involving Ledyard's fatefully late surrender and his and his men's massacre by the British occurred historically as we describe it. Jordan Freeman was there by Ledyard's side and did as we say (pp. 30-31).

The British burned the town of New London, sixty-five dwellings, thirty-one stores and warehouses, eighteen craft shops, twenty barns, the courthouse, jail, customhouse—and even the (presumably loyal) Anglican Church, because winds swept the fires out of control. Eighty Americans were killed—most of them after the surrender—and about thirty-five wounded, most of whom died. Except for a half a dozen or so who escaped, the rest

JORDAN FREEMAN SPEARS MAJOR MONTGOMERY

were taken prisoner; the badly wounded were left in New London on parole (a promise not to fight again), and the walking wounded taken to New York, but within a few weeks all were paroled and sent home. Benedict Arnold reported fifty-four British troops dead and 142 wounded—many of whom died aboard ship returning to New York.

The other episode forms the basis of not only our story about Willy Freeman but also that of Daniel Arabus in *Jump Ship to Freedom*. It involves the historically significant trial of the actual Jack Arabus. Arabus was a slave to the merchant and ship captain Thomas Ivers, who lived in that part of Stratford, Connecticut, which later became Bridgeport, a natural harbor on Long Island Sound. Slavery was legal in Connecticut, but statutes prohibited transporting slaves in or out of the state for the purpose of selling them. In January 1784 an act for gradual emancipation was adopted, but it applied only to persons born of slave mothers after March 15, 1784, and would not have affected either the historical or fictional figures in our stories.

After the first blush of Revolutionary enthusiasm, military recruitment became difficult in all states, including Connecticut. Congress and the states offered bounties as incentives, but that failed to draw enough men to fill the quotas levied by Congress. In Connecticut the quotas were parceled out to the towns, and they also offered bounties. Even this didn't provide enough men, and towns began subjecting eligible men to a draft by lottery. Apparently, one of Thomas Ivers' sons was called up, and Ivers sent his slave, Jack Arabus, in his stead and pocketed the ten-pound town bounty.

We have Arabus' military record. The name is spelled various-ly: Aribus, Arribas, Arrabus. He served in a number of Connecticut regiments—which, incidentally were fully integrat-ed—from November 1777 to some time after June 1783. When the term for which he was drafted expired, apparently six months ending in May 1778, he enlisted for the duration. It is my under-standing that Arabus would have had to have Ivers' permission to do that. When he was mustered out he returned to Stratford, where Ivers claimed him as property.

Arabus fled "eastward," was captured, and incarcerated in the county jail in New Haven. There he sought help and found it among a number of sympathetic people, among whom was Elizur Goodrich. Goodrich graduated from Yale in 1779 at the age of eighteen and served as an instructor there for a couple of years. He then read law in his uncle's office (there were no law schools in the United States until 1784) and was admitted to practice about 1784. He was then twenty-three years old. He later became an influential Federalist political figure and served in high state office and in Congress.

What we know about the trial is drawn from the official records, shown here, which are bare bones, and a brief newspa-per account. We show here the finding of the Court as given in *Root's Reports,* the official journal of Connecticut legal actions of the era. Our account of the trial follows what facts we have, though, of course, Willy was not present, there being no histori-

NEW HAVEN COUNTY ADJOURNED SUPERIOR COURT,
A. D. 1784.

ARABAS V. IVERS.

A person illegally imprisoned may be discharged upon a *habeas corpus.*

THE case was — Jack was a slave to Ivers, and enlisted into the continental army with his master's consent — served during the war, and was discharged. Ivers claimed him as his servant; Jack fled from him to the eastward, Ivers pursued him, and took him and brought him to New Haven on his return to New York, where he belonged, and for safe-keeping while he stayed at New Haven, he got the gaoler to commit Jack to prison; and upon Jack's application to the court, complaining of his being unlawfully and unjustly holden in prison, the court issued a *habeas corpus,* to bring Jack before the court; also ordering the gaoler to certify wherefore he held Jack in prison; which being done, Ivers was cited before the court; and upon a summary hearing, Jack was discharged from his imprisonment, upon the ground that he was a freeman, absolutely manumitted from his master by enlisting and serving in the army as aforesaid.

cal Willy. At least three hundred African-Americans from Connecticut served in the Revolutionary army, most had been emancipated to do so—like Jordan Freeman. But for those whose masters still claimed them as property, Arabus' case had the effect of legal emancipation. We lose sight of Jack Arabus after the trial. He does not appear on the 1790 census list for any Connecticut town. That Jordan Freeman and Jack Arabus were married to sisters is entirely fictitious; indeed, we don't even know if they were married at all.

Literary Analysis: The Themes

War Comes to Willy Freeman, as I've already explained, is the first story in the series, but was written second. Our purpose in this book is to describe the hierarchies of power that prevailed in this premodern class society. They are those of race, gender, age, and slave-master. Willy sits at the bottom of these: she is a black female child, until days before our story begins, a slave. She is very much aware of her status and comments frequently about it.

Slave-Master Relationship

The slave-master relationship is always present in this book, largely because Willy, now free, was until very recently a slave.

Willy grew up in relatively benign conditions of slavery, close enough to the free status she gains just before our story opens to have a strong sense of what both conditions were like. She had always resented her servile state and acted out her resentments through sassing her parents and arguing with authority figures. She knew "arguing like mostly I would" (p. 4) was a dangerous practice that would get her in trouble some day. And, actually, she *thinks* about arguing more often than she does it. She represses the urge to argue with her father, with Captain Ivers, with British soldiers and other officials. It is only with Horace, who tried to lord it over her after she reveals that she is a girl, with whom she argues regularly (p. 124).

As experiences strengthen Willy's character and resolve, she becomes more self-assertive. She leaves Fraunces, despite his wish that she stay. She insists on entering the Ivers' house in the face of objections by Jack Arabus. And finally she not only argues with Captain Ivers but actually attacks him physically (pp. 147-48). This was a gravely foolish act given the situation of African-Americans even in Connecticut, but one that does not surprise us in light of Willy's strong impulse toward independence. Indeed, we almost expect it. But Willy had no proof that she had been emancipated, and our fictional Ivers was not a humane character and was wholly unscrupulous when a chance to make some money appeared before his eyes. Attacking him could have had a deadly result if he'd succeeded in selling her in the West Indies.

Gender

The next of these relationships we portray is that based on sex. Willy's mother, we learn as early as page 2, "looked mighty grim and bitter, like there wasn't nothing fair in anything." That gender roles were well defined is signalled by Ma's insisting that Willy wear britches while milking, but then immediately change back to a dress. The device of having Willy wear boy's clothes throughout the story helps us point up time and again the sharp distinction between male and female roles.

That there is a power relationship between the sexes as well is iterated over and over. Jordan Freeman expects his orders to his wife—even potentially deadly ones—to be carried out. "There wasn't any going against him," Willy says. "He was the man." (p. 18) Color makes no difference in this relationship. The white Captain Ivers treats his wife in the same dominating way as does the black Jordan Freeman. "Be quiet, Mother," he says in one of his more placid moments "Don't trouble yourself with making decisions." (p. 50) "I don't want her in my house," says Mrs. Ivers. "She's staying," the Captain commands. Willy tells us, "He gave Mrs. Ivers a look. She looked mighty cross, but she didn't dare go against him." (p. 51)

Willy takes this all in. ". . . when I came to think about it, when you was a woman you was half a slave, anyway. You had to get married, otherwise you couldn't hardly support yourself, and after that your husband, he was the boss and you had to do what he said. That was so even for white women." (pp. 63-64)

The rigid gender roles apply even among children. When circumstances put Willy in close contact under great pressure with a white boy her age, she is more aware of the sex difference than the race difference. The boy, William Latham—a real character—"gave me a funny look. He knew he knew me, but dressed up like a boy the way I was he couldn't figure me out. I was going to tell him, but then suddenly it came to me that if I told him I was a girl he'd start giving me orders. . . . Of course, me being black and him white he was likely to give me orders anyway, but not so much as if I was a girl." (p. 26. See also p. 29.) Later, our character, Horace, treats Willy one way when he thinks she is a boy, and another when the truth is known. Horace curses "which was a thing he wouldn't have done if he'd know I was a girl." (p. 103) That the relationship had changed radically is demonstrated by the description of the sleeping and dressing arrangements after Horace learns that Willy is a girl. (p. 122) Finally, we show that the conventional gendered power structure could be killing, as in the disgusting conduct of the drunken man in Canvas Town (pp. 97-98).

Note that every time men discover Willy is female, she gets molested—from our peeking Horace (p. 122) to the threatened rapes (pp. 11, 75-76). But note, also, that the fact of her sex saves her life, too (pp. 33-34).

Willy notes that color doesn't seem to matter in relations between men and women. Apparently, for her, it was worse to be female than to be black. Ma points out the paradox of black men—even slaves—offering their lives in a war that would bring "freedom" only to whites (p. 9). Willy appears to have greater concern for women. ". . . it seemed to me that it was the white men who were going to come out of it on top, the way they always did. The black men, leastwise the ones who fought and got their freedom, would come out second best, and the women wouldn't be no better off than they always was." (p. 64)

Age

It is perhaps not discrete for teachers of young teenagers to raise issues of age hierarchies, but Willy is always aware of her status as a child. From the earliest pages of the book when her father orders her into a potentially lethal situation, we show this relationship. As Ma takes orders from Pa, so Willy takes orders from Ma (e.g., pp. 3-4). In dealing with Mrs. Ivers, Willy has no gender difference to contend with but has to suffer from both age and race inferiority. "I knew I shouldn't argue with her," she thinks about Mrs. Ivers, "she was a grown-up, and I was just a child." (p. 53) Willy's only triumphant moment in long years of wartime travail is her realization, invoked as the last sentence in our story, that finally, after all she had experienced and survived, "I was grown-up; and it was all going to be new." (p. 173)

Race

Willy is black, but she is no longer a slave. Her freedom is the one positive element in her life, and she is determined to hold onto it. Nothing gratifies her more than that Samuel Fraunces treats her as wage labor. And nothing terrifies her more than the prospect of being reenslaved by Thomas Ivers, who "looked me up and down like I was some kind of livestock for sale" (p. 55). Willy cringes under the equally denigrating glare of Mrs. Ivers, who "went on staring at me as if I was lower than dirt and she was afraid she'd soil herself just by looking at me." (pp. 48-49) Captain Ivers takes for granted that Willy is lying about being free and assumes that he will control her destiny: "She's staying . . . Until I decide what to do with her," he says (p. 5). Willy, in Ivers' eyes, is chattel—mere property.

The place of African-Americans at the bottom of the social hierarchy is signaled by the use of the word nigger. The word is first used by a black soldier among the British troops invading New London and Groton (p. 7). They were members of a regiment of the New Jersey Line, which was in fact part of the invasion. They allude to the official British policy of not harassing blacks in hopes of enlisting them into their army. It was, as a matter of fact, the fear that significant numbers of enslaved African-Americans might join the enemy that moved Washington and the Continental Congress to allow the enlistment of free blacks—or slaves emancipated for the purpose—into the Continental forces. But as soldiers or civilians, African-Americans were routinely referred to as niggers; it was a perpetually open sore from the wound of slavery.

Willy may have been an unusual African-American female in her efforts to realize some self-determination in a society whose attitudes and institutions denied her that right. We think, however, that she may very well be representative of at least free blacks in the North. "It was a funny thing to me how people wanted to be free. If you was scrubbing a floor for your own self in your own cabin, why, that was all right; it didn't hardly seem like work. But if you was scrubbing somebody else's floor, it was just awful." (pp. 64-65).

It is perhaps an act of projection for me and my brother, two middle-aged, middle-class white males, to believe that all people everywhere want to control their own destiny. But that is our conviction, nevertheless. Such an urge is not necessarily expressed in outright revolt. Slaves in plantation societies developed all sorts of techniques to preserve their sense of self and express at least some degree of autonomy. One of these came to be known as "puttin' on ol' massa." The idea was to appear subservient while in fact obstructing master's commands. Horace explains how to carry out these deceptions when he tells Willy, "Now the first thing about a lie is, it's got to be ordinary . . . another thing about lying, you always want to lower yourself. . . ." (p. 81. There is another example of puttin' on ol' massa in *Who Is Carrie?*, p. 91). But whatever the methods of protecting one's ego and one's self-determination, we think the urge is universal.

Willy says, "I hated having somebody over me, and I don't guess I was any different from anybody else." She could see that the war was about being free from crown and Parliament to control the nation's destiny: "I could see that people had a mighty strong feeling for being free, if they was willing to risk being shot for it." (p. 172)

But freedom, she realizes, is relative. "Of course, some people was going to be more free than others. There wasn't no way around that. Slaves wasn't going to be no freer under the Americans than they was under the British, and women was still going to have to keep their place. I was black and I was a woman, and I knew there was limits. . . . I could see nobody was free all the way." (p. 172)

Willy is uncommonly thoughtful about the social hierarchy in which "if you was black, you was down at the bottom." (p. 64) Gender and race, Willy sees, will determine her life's course unless she is able to escape society's bounds. "I would have to take orders as long as I lived." She could look forward to a change in the hierarchy only in God's community: "Maybe in heaven black folks gave orders to white folks and women gave orders to men." (p. 72) This thought, at first only a fantasy, hints at Willy's future course, however. While accepting the hierarchy, she is determined to avoid being reenslaved, and beyond that, to gain some control over her own destiny.

Willy's efforts to be reunited with her mother are truly heroic. Setting off down Long Island Sound in a small sailboat at night was an act of extraordinary daring. Her clever escape from the whaleboat raiders (an episode, incidentally, that follows many such actual events), required, not only bravery, but also a high order of imagination and intelligence. She shows initiative and courage, too, in bringing her problems to Samuel Fraunces in that deferential society, for it "was pretty bold for somebody low as me to go marching up to somebody has high as Mr. Fraunces." (p. 84) And most of all, her expedition into Canvas Town, a place, in fact, even more dangerous and frightening than we have described it—would have intimidated the roughest and biggest men.

It is especially when she leaves Fraunces Tavern to try to save her mother—at the risk of falling into Captain Ivers' hands—that Willy shows her determination to command her own life. This action leads finally to a legal confirmation of her free status, and validates all those efforts symbolized by her name—which reflects the will to be free.

Jump Ship To Freedom

Introduction

For many years my teaching responsibilities included courses on both early American history and United States constitutional history. These two specialties grew out of my doctoral dissertation, which was a life-and-times biography of Roger Sherman (1721-93), a significant Connecticut politician who, among other accomplishments, was a member of the five-man committee that wrote the Declaration of Independence and a very influential member of the Constitutional Convention of 1787. That interest would generate an adult nonfiction book, *Decision In Philadelphia*, coauthored with James, published at the time of the bicentennial of that Convention. It made sense to employ my special knowledge about the origins of the Constitution in one of our young adult novels.

The era of the 1960s and 1970s was one in which a tremendous amount of public concern was focused on the problem of race in America. Both my brother and I were involved in various ways in the black civil rights movement of those decades. Civil rights in the United States are constitutionally based, and a book about the relationship of the creation of the Constitution to slavery seemed a socially useful project for the times. Slaves, though not necessarily free blacks, were no better off after the Constitution was put in place than before—indeed, they were probably worse off, at least in the short run, perhaps until 1863.

As I have already explained, *Jump Ship to Freedom* was to have been a stand-alone book; there was no thought while we were writing it that it would become the middle volume of a trilogy. Our working title for it was "the constitution book," and that accurately suggests the historical focus we worked with.

Two of our earlier works, *The Bloody Country* and *The Winter Hero,* had explored the problems of a central government that merely "confederated" the "sovereign states" in a loose relationship under the Articles of Confederation. That first constitution delegated no taxing or coercive power to the Congress, and the cohesiveness and viability of the United States was threatened at every turn on virtually a daily basis. *Jump Ship to Freedom* addresses the extreme ends of the continuum from slavery to freedom. Governments—state and national in a federal system—that had the authority and effective power to protect individual freedoms were brought into being only by sanctioning the institution of slavery and the perpetual bondage of individual slaves.

Our narrator, Daniel Arabus, finds himself in the intellectually and emotionally wrenching position of having to decide between the immediate freedom of himself and his mother, and the long-term prospect for slavery as an institution. One course of action would perpetuate the institution, but gain his own freedom; another course might weaken the institution, but also diminish the prospect of freedom for himself and his mother. "On the one hand," he puzzles, "they'd bargained us blacks into slavery forever. On the other hand, if there was no bargain, maybe there'd be no new government and my soldiers' notes wouldn't be worth a penny." (p. 139. See also pp. 159, 167.)

The Historical Context

Jump Ship To Freedom takes place in 1787. The setting is that part of Stratford, Connecticut, that is now Bridgeport. The house we

PHOTO BY JILL BURDEN

assign to Thomas Ivers was in fact built in 1787 by Ivers' stepson John Brooks, a fourth-generation ship captain. The Brooks family descendants lived in the house until 1961 when the last of them died. The house, then the only remaining 18th-century structure in Bridgeport, was given to the local historical society. John Brooks

PHOTO BY JILL BURDEN

was the actual captain of the *Junius Brutus*. The house, until the 1970s located near the water in East Bridgeport, was dismantled and reconstructed on the grounds of the Discovery Museum about three miles inland. It is once again falling into disrepair as these pictures, taken in April 1998, show. The house was located at what is now the corner of Stratford Avenue (Route 130 on the inset) and Pembroke Street. That is the location of the more inland of the buildings labeled Brooks on the 18th-century map. The other building, I believe, is the Brooks warehouse. This is a fragment of a map drawn by the British military about 1778 to guide them in their raids along the Connecticut Coast.

The central episode of our story is the writing of the draft constitution between May and September 1787. The final constitution reflected a great number of compromises, large and small, made by delegates representing different philosophies of government, different economic and political interests, and even different individual personalities. We focus on two concerns: the status of the slave trade (not slavery itself) and fugitive slaves under the Constitution; and the fiscal measures instituted by the new government provided for by the Constitution.

The Framers did not consider the abolition of slavery. Not more than a half a dozen of the fifty-five men at the Convention wanted such a thing; everyone knew that there would be no Constitution without sanctioning and practicing the institution of slavery. The importation of slaves from foreign places was a dif-

ferent matter. Even some
Southerners wanted to end
that trade; some for
social and moral con-
cerns, some for eco-
nomic reasons, some
for all of these.
Many—perhaps
most—Northerners
found the slave trade
morally repugnant
and would like
to see it
stopped.
B u t

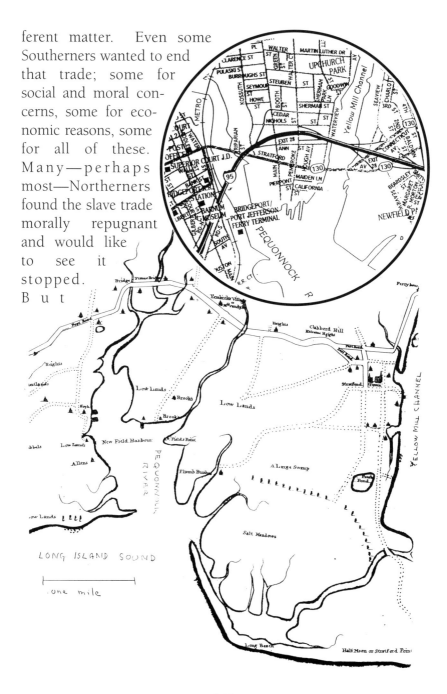

LONG ISLAND SOUND

one mile

they soon discovered, if they didn't know it already, that the three Deep South states—the Carolinas and Georgia—would not federate if the foreign slave trade was forbidden. (There was no talk of interfering with buying and selling slaves within states or across state lines.)

Our plot is built around the unfolding of an immensely complex set of compromises involving the regulation of trade including that in slaves, the legitimation of crossing state lines to capture fugitive slaves, and the future of slavery in the western lands. (We explain this in bits and pieces, but lay out the basis of it on pages 136-138; see also pp. 159, 167.) The last of these concerns was resolved by the Northwest Ordinance of 1787 enacted by Congress sitting in New York within days of the adoption by the delegates in Philadelphia of the fugitive slave clause that appears in Article IV, Section 2, of the Constitution. It is this clause that we focus on in *Jump Ship to Freedom.* The section reads: "No person held to Service or Labour in one State, under the Laws thereof, escaping into another, shall, in Consequence of any Law or Regulation therein, be discharged from such Service or Labour, but shall be delivered up on Claim of the Party to whom such Service or Labour may be due." This section and legislation implementing it remained the law of the land until obviated by the Constitution's Thirteenth Amendment, which ended slavery in 1865.

Other elements of the Constitution affected by sectional compromises brought about the system by which representation and direct taxation were to be apportioned. Three-fifths of the slaves were to be counted. No restriction on the foreign slave trade would be permitted for at least twenty years, and by implication other provisions recognized slavery as a constitutionally sanctioned institution. By helping to bring about these features of the Constitution, our Daniel betrays the interests of his fellow slaves.

The second strand of our historical theme is the one that justifies Daniel's decision. If the compromises are not concluded, the Convention will break up, the Union will probably collapse, and the United States notes (in our fictional account worth $600) will pass from nearly valueless to totally valueless. Dan will not be able to buy the freedom of his mother and himself. I have explained the fiscal background of these notes in my analysis of the economic themes in *The Winter Hero.* (pp. 98-99 above)

The narrative of the second half of *Jump Ship to Freedom* relies on the fact that sixteen of the fifty-five delegates at the Convention at Philadelphia were also members of Congress sitting in New York and often traveled between the two bodies. It was this inter-communication that made possible the sharing of information and bargaining that brought about compromises, some elements of which were enacted into ordinances by Congress and other elements of which were more or less simultaneously adopted by the delegates in Philadelphia. The fascinating detective work that uncovered these maneuvers was done by Staughton Lynd in the essay listed in the bibliography below and explained in Chapter 15 of our own *Decision in Philadelphia.* Our concluding episode involving Alexander Hamilton and George Washington is entirely fanciful. The grain of truth in it is that the message about the compromise effected in New York was probably carried to Philadelphia by Hamilton or a fellow traveler, Manasseh Cutler who arrived together on July 12.

The issues before the Framers in Philadelphia in 1787 included much more than the future of slavery and the slave trade, of course. The central issue before the Convention was federalism—the division of powers between the state and national governments. We approach this matter only tangentially through the fact of interstate import duties—the impost (pp. 75-76, 80). We have Captain Ivers facing the prospect of paying duties on goods imported into New York. In fact, it had been rumored in 1786 that Connecticut and New Jersey were on the verge of launching troops against New York to stop this drain on their economies. In *The Bloody Country,* we have shown the actuality of war between two states—Connecticut and Pennsylvania. It was interstate disturbances such as these—and local insurrections like Shays'

Rebellion described in *The Winter Hero*—that moved the Framers to write a constitution providing for a strong central government. The slavery issue was secondary, and tended to divide rather than unite the Framers. But teachers dealing with the reasons for calling the Philadelphia Convention of 1787 will find these New York imposts a good starting point.

Chronology

Opening scene, June 17, 1787
Leave Newfield, June 18
Storm at Sea, June 24-28
Start to NYC, June 29
Arrive NYC, July 6
At Fraunces Tavern, July 7-10
Leave NYC, July 10
Arrive Philadelphia, July 12

Literary Analysis

The central element of *Jump Ship to Freedom,* of course, is Dan's awakening to the meaninglessness of skin color and the cruel misconceptions of stereotypes. We develop this theme in large measure through Dan's changing self-image, symbolized by the word nigger.

Dan has categorized himself according to society's dictates, and as our story opens castigates himself as a stupid nigger—indeed, stupid *because* he is a nigger (p. 2). "But I was black," he thinks, "and wasn't as smart as white folks." Then, reflecting the social context of his thoughts, he adds, "Leastwise, that's what Mr. Leaming, the minister, always said. . . ." (p. 2) ". . . that was God's way. . . . Black folks were meant to do the work, and white folks the thinking." (pp. 4-5) Well past the midpoint of our narrative, Daniel still has thoughts "about how much smarter white folks are

THE PICTURE HERE SHOWS SECOND STREET IN PHILADELPHIA AS DAN MIGHT HAVE SEEN IT IN 1787. BEHIND THE BUILDING WITH THE MANSARD ROOF, RISES THE TOWER ATOP THE STATE HOUSE (NOW INDEPENDENCE HALL) WHERE THE CONSTITUTION WAS WRITTEN.

than black." (p. 94) And on the very eve of his self-affirmation, he is still capable of characterizing himself as a "stupid nigger." (p. 116)

But right from the start, there is a hint of doubt about this virtually universal stereotype: ". . . when you got down to it," Daniel ruminates, "my daddy was pretty smart, and he was black." (p. 2) Dan begins to realize the falsity of the stereotype when Mr. Fatherscreft remarks to him, "Seems to me you had to be pretty smart . . ." (p. 116) "Thou're clearly an intelligent and resourceful boy." (p. 135) But of greater impact than white men's words are Daniel's actions themselves. Through an extraordinary series of self-determined events, Daniel has evinced loyalty, integrity, intelligence, bravery—in short, strength of character. He risks reenslavement on the basis of his loyalty to his mother as well as in his own interest. And again, he shows the profoundest integrity in keeping a death bed promise. His high intelligence is demonstrated in many instances, but none more telling than his ability to understand and memorize the compromise that saved the Constitution. Thus, finally, Daniel purges his mind of the stereotype imposed on the basis of race. ". . . it seems to me there ain't much difference one way or another. You take my daddy, and Big Tom and Mr. Ivers and Birdsey and me, and take the skin off us, and it would be pretty hard to tell which was the white ones and which ones wasn't." (p. 187)

Throughout our story, Daniel is inspired by the memory of his father. At every dark moment, Jack Arabus appears in Daniel's thoughts and spurs the boy on to reject defeat and forge ahead. Right from the start we know that Daniel thought "daddy was pretty smart," (p. 2) and "about the bravest man there ever was." (p. 5) At his most depressed moments when he felt "all cold and lonely," the picture of Daddy would come into Daniel's head. "He sure wouldn't have taken no pride in me if I just up and quit the whole thing," for even in death, "I wanted him to be proud of me." (pp. 50-51)

Imprisoned in the Captain's quarters on the *Junius Brutus* soon to be sold off in the West Indies, with nowhere to turn and no one to talk to, Dan is about to give up. "Then all at once in my head I saw my daddy standing up staring down at me. I looked at him, and he looked at me. . . . . . He was thinking that if he'd been in my fix, he wouldn't have laid there on his back feeling sorry for himself. He'd have got up and done something about it." (p. 85). And so Dan does, engineering his escape and ultimately his and his mother's freedom. Again and again (pp. 124, 144, 163, 183) Daddy's image inspires Daniel to greater effort and new heights of perseverance, courage, and ingenuity. The theme of father as mentor and inspiration is perhaps the strongest in the book.

The *Junius Brutus* is so called because that in fact was the name of the ship that made the harrowing storm-driven voyage we write about, the log of which provided the detail of our description.

But there is unintended irony here because Junius Brutus was a 16th-century Protestant revolutionary, the author of a tract called *Vindiciae Contra Tyrannos* (*A Defense of Liberty Against Tyrants*, 1579). Yet here, the *Junius Brutus* is a floating prison for Daniel, carrying the boy to lifelong slavery without hope of liberation. The only extant ship I could find that resembled the *Junius Brutus* was the Beaver II, a 19th-century vessel reconstructed to resemble the famous Boston Tea Party ship, anchored today as a floating museum in Boston Harbor. It is depicted on the cover of *Jump Ship*.

In *The Bloody Country* we juxtapose human values and property values and suggest that a balance of them must be struck in order to gain a truly fulfilling life. In *Jump Ship to Freedom* we try to show that human life—at least a life in freedom—cannot be given a monetary value. Captain and Mrs. Ivers are set up as personifying the mercenary spirit. Symbolically, this is portrayed when Mrs. Ivers hides the Arabus' soldiers' notes in her Bible over which she prays each evening (p. 4). The Captain risks lives, and loses some, when he refuses to jettison the cargo to save the ship and its crew. He sees all of life's affairs in mercenary terms. Dan is not so much a person as he is a piece of property worth £80, no more than "a hog ready for butchering." (p. 27)

For Dan, the perspective is the opposite. As Dan represents cash to Ivers, so the soldiers' notes represent liberty to Dan. When Fatherscreft exclaims that he would have thought Dan would be worth more than £80 to himself, Dan is forced to ponder the issue and conclude, "Well, I guess a man's life don't exactly measure out in money. I mean, what's the use of having the money, if you don't have your life?" (p. 111) Then the old white Quaker and the young black slave turn to a discussion of the soldiers' notes—both symbol and potential reality of freedom for Dan, a point he had acknowledged from the start: for Mum and Daniel, "those soldiers' notes . . . was freedom." (p. 6)

Documents: *Junius Brutus Log*

One of the most exciting sources I used in devising *Jump Ship* was the collection of Brooks Family papers at the Discovery Museum in Bridgeport, Connecticut. John Brooks was a fourth-generation sea captain plying the trade between Long Island Sound and the Caribbean islands. His journals, account books, and the ship's logs are at the Museum.

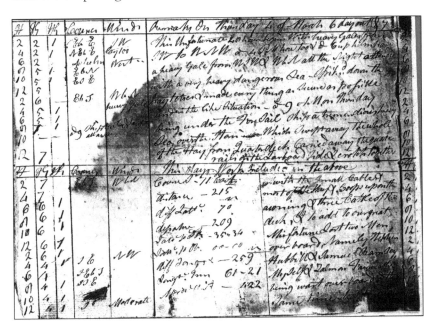

The log includes the incredible account of the storm in which four men were washed overboard but then two were hauled back on board. In our story, two go over, one comes back (pp. 71-72).

John Brooks' log of the *Junius Brutus*

3 Mar Very heavy winds "The most Alarmming unfortunate time that I ever yet had for poor stock. The day ends with a heavy blow from SWS ..."
Mar 4 Thurs - [sixth day out] "This Unfortunate 48 hours

began with heavy Gales from SW to WNW at 4 P.M. hove too at 6 [uphelm?] had a heavy Gale from WSW & W to N all the Night attended with a very heavy dangerous Sea—Spiked down the hatches & made everything as Secure as possible under the like Situation—at 9 AM on Thursday being under the foreSail ship'd a tremendous heavy Sea over the Main Which Swept away the whole the Hay from Quarterdeck Carried away the quarter rails on the Larboard Side & Crotch together with the small Cables & most of the Hay & Coops. Upon the awning & three Cattle of[f] the deck, & to add to our great Misfortunate Los two Men over board, Namely Stephen Hubbill & James Ramsey, Myself & Zalmon Fairweather being warst overboard at the same time but through Gods distinguishing Mercy we were Got inboard—by the assistance of those on deck. in the Meantime the brigg came round head to the wind & Shipt no Sea till we got her befor it again which we found very difficult to do as the tiller was broke short off in the rudder head, we however with the assistance of an ax cut it out & weather'd the Gale after lighting [throwing overboard] After decks of all the Hay & the Remaining Coops in the awning together with 10 head of Cattle, which was done as soon as possible after getting her before the wind at about herd[n] the Gale still encreased and rais'd a Most Mountainous [leomeing?] Sea in which we found the Brigg Was not able to possible to Weather it, we for the preservation of our own Lives & the remaining part of the Cargo, lighted her decks of 8 head of Cattle more which amounted to 18 however 3 Wast away total 21 head lost at about 12 AM on Thursday Night it seem'd to rather Moderate and incline to the Northward, So that after a very fatguing time through Gods grace & Mercy we were preserved for which blessed be his Holy Name"

[Heavy rains & sea the next day. Did not clear up till Friday March 2—14th day out] at 7 on Monday Morning May 17th Arriv'd Safe to anchor at Newfield where begun and Ends this unfortunate Voayge—all Well On Board Thanks be to God

Who Is Carrie?

Historical Context

On June 21, 1788, New Hampshire became the ninth state to ratify the new U.S. Constitution, thus securing the number agreed upon to effectuate it. In June and July, New York and Virginia ratified, bringing in two essential states. On September 13 the old Congress under the Articles of Confederation set the date for the appointment (in any manner each state legislature chose) of presidential electors as January 7, and established the site for the meeting of the new government as New York, where the old Congress was in session. The electors met on February 4, 1789, and unanimously chose George Washington president and, with thirty-four votes out of sixty-nine, John Adams became vice president. On April 1, 1789, the House of Representatives organized itself, and five days later the Senate did so.

Our story of Carrie begins on April 23 with Washington's much celebrated arrival in New York City and then a week later, with Washington's inaugural on the balcony of Federal Hall—(New York's former City Hall)—on Wall Street, shown here. This is Broad Street facing City Hall, where Washington was sworn in on the balcony. Entering on the left is Pearl Street, the site of Fraunces Tavern. Washington was sworn in by Robert R. Livingston, chancellor of New York (roughly, chief justice). The presidential mansion was on Cherry Street, about where the foundation of the Brooklyn Bridge is today. Of course, the major legislative events of the First Congress were the adoption of the amendments that became the Bill of Rights when ratified by the states, and the very important Judiciary Act of 1789. The issues central to our story, however, center on Treasury Secretary Alexander Hamilton's fiscal program.

This program included legislation that would refinance the national debt, usually referred to as the Funding Plan, and another arrangement to have the new government pay off the debts the states had incurred during the course of the Revolution. This was called the Assumption Plan. Funding and assumption would enhance the value of all the various kinds of paper notes the states and Congress had issued. Rumors of the progress and lack of progress of these bills through Congress caused the value of the notes to rise and fall. These matters were not resolved for two years, but in 1791 our fictional Daniel would be able to redeem his father's soldiers' notes and buy freedom for himself and his mother. The notes were paid off at face value with accrued interest, so that Dan would have received much more than $600. We refer to these fiscal plans at various points in our story; the fullest discussion is on pages 33-34. The funding and assumption plans were passed by Congress in July and August 1790.

An associated issue plaguing the First Congress was a permanent location for the government. Places as dispersed as Hartford and Richmond were in the mix, with Northerners working for a northern location and Southerners a southern one. Since the assumption was favored more by Northerners and opposed by Virginians, Hamilton of New York struck a bargain with Secretary of State Thomas Jefferson in a famous conference on the steps of the presidential mansion, just as we portray it (pp. 141-42). Jefferson agreed to persuade his following in Congress to support assumption and Hamilton agreed to support a southern site for the government. Maryland had already offered a tract ten miles square on the Potomac just across from Alexandria, Virginia, where Washington's Mount Vernon was located. This Maryland site became Washington, D.C. Part of this bargain had the government leaving New York City and locating temporarily in Philadelphia (p. 63), which it did on December 6, 1790. The government moved to the District of Columbia in 1800.

Article IV, Section 2, of the U.S. Constitution was the now infamous fugitive slave provision that was part of the bargain made between Southerners and Northerners that I have described in my discussion of the historical context of *Jump Ship to Freedom*. The text of it is there (pp. 145 above). Under the Articles of Confederation, states were free to protect runaway slaves from masters or alleged masters—or their agents—who crossed state bounds to capture them. There was no requirement that state governments encourage or even permit assistance in recapture efforts. Under the Constitution, however, officials of governments in free, as well as slave, states were required to "deliver up" real or alleged runaways.

Though this section of the Constitution was not implemented by legislation until enactment of the Fugitive Slave Act of 1793, an active practice of kidnapping (the word they used) free blacks as well as recapturing runaway slaves flourished. No one knows, of course, the number of free African-Americans captured for sale in the South or the West Indies, but it was in the thousands. Northern states attempted to thwart kidnapping by legislation, judicial rules and actions, and by local police ordinances. But the practice continued. Our fictional Carrie, a young female of problematic status, would have been a prime target even if Captain Ivers had not been in our fictional picture. Her pursuer's hands smell like tar (p. 20), an indication that he is probably a sailor. Perhaps it is Big Tom himself.

Literary Analysis

In *War Comes to Willy Freeman* we sought to portray the place of blacks in American society during the Revolutionary Era. Willy was not a slave during the time of our story, but had been until weeks, or perhaps only days, before it began. Her experiences reflect not only those of an African-American of the time but also of a female. *Jump Ship to Freedom* deals with the relationship of African-Americans to the Constitution and makes the point that enslaved blacks were worse off after the Constitution went into effect than before. Note, for instance, Daniel's ironic remark during the letter-writing scene with Horace, "Do as you like, Horace, it's a free country." (p. 75) Of course, the word "mighty" could not be spelled any way Horace liked even though Horace was free. The irony is that though the United States was supposed to be a free country, Daniel, as he spoke these words, was a slave. It is Carrie's uncertain status that forms the central theme of our story. Carrie does not know who her parents are, but unlike Harriet Beecher Stowe's Topsy, she is not content to accept the explanation that she "just growed." Her incomplete biography gnaws away at her, not only because a full knowledge might set her free but also because she needs a complete persona in order to have a full sense of self.

Carrie's lack of a known heritage and fixed culture is, of course, a metaphor for her race. America's black slaves, wrenched from their African homelands and their families, transported to an alien and hostile society, and held in physical and intellectual bondage, had been separated from their parents, spouses, and all other peole in their extended families. They had also lost much—if not most—of their culture, and retained only infrequent and diluted connections with it. Efforts by African-Americans over the past couple of generations to revitalize lost cultures and family heritage make poignantly clear how deeply felt that loss has been. Carrie's soul-felt response to her heartrending predicament is supposed to embody the yearning of both free and slave black Americans of her era. Carrie's anguished cries, in the closing words of the book, give voice to the central characteristic of slavery then and racism now.

Who Is Carrie? tries to convey the utter desperation—psychological, emotional, and physical felt by an intelligent and energetic young girl held in bondage. The core of Carrie's desperation is her need to know who she is, not so much because the answer might release her from the bonds of slavery but principally for psychological peace of mind. The title of the book, of course, reflects that theme.

We establish Carrie's character in *Jump Ship to Freedom,* where her curiosity—an indication of her intelligence and imagination—earns her the nickname Nosey. The name Carrie, of course, signals her position as a servant who spends so much of her time in fetching and carrying. Significantly, she knows of no surname; but by the end of the story she will believe—and we will suspect—that it is Freeman, which, of course, carries its own symbolic weight. The curiosity theme permeates the book and is demonstrated in the opening paragraphs. Explaining why she was so strongly impelled to risk punishment in order to watch Washington's inaugural parade, she says, "It was just my dinged curiosity. I couldn't stand for anything to happen without me being in on it. It's why they called me Nosey." (p. 2) We know that this curiosity will get her into trouble as often as not. But at base it is the result of not knowing who she is.

Carrie's inquisitiveness, then, was not idle curiosity: At its root lay a profound and abiding need to understand her situation and more especially where she came from. She was missing that biography that most of us take for granted and that gives us a sense of self and a connection to our past and to our present social context. The book tells a mystery story. As Carrie says, "I was a mystery to my self." But a very painful mystery. "Sometimes when I thought about it, it made me feel so sick and low I'd near bust out crying." Then she articulates the core insight of the book: "If you didn't know who you was, you wasn't nobody. There ain't nothing much worse than being nobody." (p. 11)

As slavery went, Carrie lived under just about the most benign conditions of any enslaved African in America. The contrast of her life with those of field hands in the sugar and rice swamps of the Deep South could hardly be greater. This helps us make the point that slavery even under the most humane and caring conditions was still terrible. "Oh, it was hard not having no choice about things and being at everybody's mercy, and not having no life of my own. I was at the bottom: there wasn't nobody lower than me, not even the tavern dogs. They could run off through the streets whenever they wanted to, or just lay around in front of the fire if they wanted to do that. They didn't work neither, but got their food whether they done anything for it or not. It was hard being worse off than dogs." (p. 94)

To fill this awful hole in Carrie's heart, she had, at the very least, to know who she was. "It didn't matter to Dan if I didn't know who my Ma and Pa was, but I *had* to know. I just *had* to know." (p. 50) She would risk everything to avoid "going through life never knowin' who I was and just being nobody at all." (p. 81)

Without a real biography to give Carrie some emotional and psychological base, she spends her hours in daydreams and fantasies. These are not self-aggrandizing like the tall tales Horace spins about himself, but rather wistful dreams of a better life and more comforting human relationships. She empathizes with animals, putting herself in their place. Watching birds, she thinks, "That's what I'd do if I could fly—go way, way up and look down, and see the whole of New York City all at once, the buildings so tiny and the people no bigger than cockroaches." But reality is never far off: "I'd give anything to have wings. I'd fly away and never be a slave no more." (p. 39)

Kids of the age we write for have a very strong sense of justice and we play on this strenuously in our effort to convey the horrible injustice of slavery. The use of the word nigger should communicate some of the degradation of slavery. As Carrie notes, in society's eyes, she "was just cargo like boxes and bags." (p. 24) Carrie knows the system is not fair and living in a society with few slaves, surrounded on a daily and close basis with not only free whites like the cooks but also free blacks like Horace, she could

BROAD STREET IN NEW YORK (1797). FRAUNCES TAVERN WAS AT THE FAR END ON THE LEFT.

rarely escape the contrast. We make this point over and over. Daily contact with the cooks and Horace brings daily discouragement. "It wasn't fair; but there wasn't anything I could do about that, either." (p. 12) "It's what you got for being black—the whites could do anything they wanted to and you couldn't say nothing about it. It ain't fair." (p. 49) And finally Carrie's heartfelt and heartrending wail that ends our story. "It isn't fair, Dan. It isn't fair." (p. 147)

This particular ending deserves some emphasis and explanation since it was not developed easily. For one thing, it is terribly unsatisfying. Young readers may even feel some of the wrenching frustration that Carrie evinces here. But, of course, we intend that. However, we had written several other endings, always with the happy discovery of papers proving that Lucy Freeman was Carrie's mother and testifying to her free status. We hint at this very, very broadly when we describe the circumstances of Carrie's mother when Jack Arabus delivered her to Fraunces. Those were exactly the circumstances of Willy's mother. (p. 119) The problem with these "happy" endings is that they obscured the larger picture we were trying to draw: that of the horrors of slavery—even in the North; even under the most benign of circumstances. *War Comes to Willy Freeman* ended triumphally—though in a gravely Pyrrhic victory, for Willy's mother and father were dead, and she was a fugitive. It was a satisfying conclusion, nevertheless. In *Jump Ship to Freedom,* though Dan has had to make a fateful choice fraught with ill omens, and sees freedom only as a long term potentiality, the story still ends with mission accomplished. Such affirmative conclusions do not convey the reality of black lives in Revolutionary America. It was essential to our didactic objective that the Arabus Trilogy end in this vividly ambiguous way.

In a poignant disquisition on what Jeffersonians would teach us to call a meritocracy, Carrie points out the inhumane arbitrariness of race-based slavery. We include this soliloquy in a scene portraying the famous Hamilton-Jefferson bargain about the Assumption Bill and the relocation of the capital to the South in hopes that teachers will make this an opportunity to discuss the anomaly of slavery in a meritocratic society (to say nothing of a "free" one). Observing the six-foot-four Jefferson in conversation with the five-foot-seven Hamilton, Carrie philosophizes:

> It was funny to see them together, for Mr. Jefferson, he was very tall and Mr. Hamilton was very short and hardly come up to Mr. Jefferson's chin. But no matter, he was just as important as Mr. Jefferson.
>
> I wondered about that. How come tall folks wasn't more important than short folks? White folks was

more important than black folks, but white folks hadn't done nothing to make themselves white any more than tall folks had to make themselves tall. It didn't seem to me that someone should be more important just because of how they was born. You ought to *do* something to get important. (p. 58)

Finally, it must be said that Carrie was not just smart and sensitive, she was also very plucky. Over and over she puts herself at risk, driven by her inner need to know who she is. In *Jump Ship to Freedom,* Dan's will is strengthened by the example of and pride in his father and by his own strong sense of honor and integrity. Carrie has no such mentor or inspiration. She has to be self-motivated, and is. "Nobody was going to help me whether I cried a bucketful or went around laughing and singing all day. The only person who would help me was myself. . . . The main person I could count on was me. And suddenly I resolved that I *would* get out of my mess somehow. I would figure out a way somehow; and I wouldn't stop until I'd done it." (p. 94) Here is a counterthematic hint. There is a real Carrie with heart and soul and guts, even if she doesn't know it yet. We know that despite everything, Carrie will persevere. And in the end, though perhaps it's just another of her fantasies, by strength of will Carrie believes she has discovered who she is, and "Oh, there wasn't no feeling in the world like that. Just like that, I wasn't nobody no more." (p. 135) But of course, she was still enslaved. There was no fairness to it.

Arabus Trilogy: Bibliography

Allyn, Charles. *The Battle of Groton Heights: A Collection of Narratives.* . . . New London, Conn.: pub. by the author, 1882. This is the best source in print for a study of Groton and the battle that opens *War Comes to Willy Freeman.* Shorter, more accessible accounts are in Boatner and Ward below.

Barck, Oscar Theodore, Jr. *New York City During the War for Independence.* New York: Columbia University Press, 1931. A treasure trove of detail about buildings, streets, British soldiers, etc.

Boatner, Mark Mayo, III. *Encyclopedia of the American Revolution*. New York: David McKay Company, 1966. The account of the Battle of Groton Heights is on pages 787-88.

Collier, Christopher, and James L. *Decision at Philadelphia: The Constitutional Convention of 1787*. New York: Random House, 1985. (Paperback ed., Ballantine, 1986). Chapter 15 includes discussion of the Lynd thesis about Congress and Convention trade-offs.

. *The American Revolution, 1763-1783* and *Creating the Constitution* in "The Drama of American History." Tarrytown, N.Y.: Marshall Cavendish, 1998.

Decatur, Stephen, Jr. *Private Affairs of George Washington From the Records and Accounts of Tobias Lear.* . . . Boston, Houghton Mifflin Company, 1933. Much detail on life at the presidential mansion on Cherry Street in New York City.

Elkins, Stanley, and Eric McKitrick. *The Age of Federalism: The Early American Republic, 1788-1800*. New York: Oxford University Press, 1993. The standard scholarly treatment of the era.

Lynd, Staughton. *Class Conflict, Slavery and the United States Constitution*. Indianapolis: The Bobbs-Merrill Company, 1967. Chapter 8, "The Compromise of 1787," outlines the thesis that informs our story in *Jump Ship to Freedom*.

Miller, John C. *The Federalist Era, 1789-1801*. New York: Harper and Brothers, 1960. An older briefer account of the years of our story in *Who Is Carrie?*.

Morris, Richard B. *The Forging of the Union, 1781-1789*. New York: Harper and Row, 1987. An easy to read authoritative account of the Confederation period by one of its foremost scholars.

Morris, Thomas D. *Freemen All: The Personal Liberty Laws of the North, 1780-1861*. Baltimore: Johns Hopkins University Press, 1974. The Personal Liberty laws were passed to prevent the kidnapping of African-Americans. This is our major source on kidnapping as told in *Who Is Carrie?*.

Rice, Kym S. *Early American Taverns: For the Entertainment of Friends and Strangers*. Chicago: Regnery Gateway, 1983. This is about taverns in general, but the principal focus is on Fraunces Tavern. There is a whole chapter on Fraunces himself.

Ward, Christopher, *The War of the Revolution*. New York: The Macmillan Company, 1952. The Battle of Groton Heights, the last military action of the Revolution in the North, was not a very significant battle and is omitted from most accounts of the war. There is a brief account on pages 626-28.

White, David O. *Connecticut's Black Soldiers, 1775-1783*. Chester, Conn.: Pequot Press, 1973. A short work that briefly discusses Jack Arabus and provides the context for his military service and his case in court.

VIII. The Clock

Historical Context

It is customary among historians to mark the beginnings of industrialism in America with the establishment of Samuel Slater's cotton mill in Pawtucket, Rhode Island, in 1790. From the moment Slater introduced water-powered spindles, which had been developed in England, to American capitalists, mills and factories began to proliferate across the countryside with amazing speed.

The embargo against foreign trade laid by the Jefferson administration in 1807 cut off imports of English textiles and gave local entrepreneurs a strong impetus to establish cotton and wool spinning and weaving mills. The embargo ruined New England overseas commerce, but at the same time provided a new opening for capital investment—the so-called "ships to spindles" movement.

Among these eager capitalists was David Humphreys of Derby, Connecticut (1752-1818; Yale, 1771). Humphreys was one of those youths known as the Hartford or Connecticut Wits who gave the new nation its first literary fillip. He had a brilliant military career during the Revolution and was a lieutenant colonel and aide-de-camp to Washington at twenty-eight. After the war, he went to Europe with Benjamin Franklin to help negotiate commercial treaties. In 1796 Humphreys was sent to Madrid as U.S. minister to Spain. Here he learned of the fine-fibered merino wool, and was inspired to bring some of these sheep to New England. He brought in a hundred merinos in 1802 and sold some of them to local farmers. The merino wool was so superior

to that of local sheep that a merino craze swept the nation, and soon the sheep were selling for as much as three thousand dollars each. Many more of these Spanish sheep were imported, and inevitably the bubble burst, leaving scores of speculators and profligate farmers at a considerable loss.

At the turn of the century, Humphreys began his career as an industrialist, first by purchasing conventional water-powered saw and fulling mills at the falls in the Naugatuck River in a part of Derby that came to be called Humphreysville (set off and incorporated as the town of Seymour in 1850). In 1806 Humphreys constructed the first textile factory in Connecticut—distinguished

from the simple mills by its combination of several processes of textile manufacture under one roof. The building, pictured here in a photograph taken in the 1870s after much alteration, was still standing in 1902. On a visit to England, Humphreys hired John Winterbotham, an accomplished textile engineer, to supervise the projected factory. A daughter of Winterbotham, Ann S. Stephens (1813-86), became a prolific writer and editor of short stories and novels. She has left memoirs of her childhood in Humphreysville and at least one novel, *Bertha's Engagement*, (1875), about the village. The novel is loaded with contemporaneous detail, much of which we have used in *The Clock*.

Humphreys imported orphan boys—at one time as many as one hundred fifty of them—from New York City and provided them with not only labor and dormitory space but also evening classes, a church, shops, and other amenities. He also organized them into a military company and bought them uniforms. The boys themselves put on plays with vernacular dialogue and left a glossary of 1810 slang used in their theatricals. With the introduction of the slubbing billies, Humphreys began employing girls in his factory, the first industrialist in Connecticut to do so.

Humphreys' mill at first included machine carding, that is, the cleaning of raw wool, described in *The Clock* (p. 24) as a dreary, even painful hand process; fulling—washing the woven fabric which was heavy with natural oil and other debris; and spinning, also described in its manual phase by Annie (p. 25). The yarn was at first put out with local farmers who did some weaving when not otherwise occupied—a method called the "putting out" system—but later done on water-driven looms in Humphreys' factory.

Derby is located at the point where the rapid-running Naugatuck River flows into the Housatonic, which in turn empties into Long Island Sound, Connecticut's southern limit. The village at the confluence, called Derby Landing—about ten miles from the Sound—was a busy port serving many sloops, brigs, and other craft employed in the West Indian and coastal trade. Ships

made regular runs to New York City, an easy overnight round-trip from Derby. Humphreys' factory was about five miles north of Derby Landing on the Naugatuck at a natural drop called Rimmon Falls. The natural falls went about two-thirds of the way across the river and was completed by a dam built in the late 18th century. The woodcut shown here was done in 1838. The artist identifies the building in the center, four stories high, as the Humphreysville Cotton Mill. Note the falls to the left.

Connecticut's textile industry was actually concentrated in the eastern part of the state near the Rhode Island border, but Humphreys' fabrics had a national reputation for quality. Humphreys' birthplace, about four miles south of the house we describe in *The Clock,* stands in what is now the town of Ansonia as a museum where one can watch costumed interpreters spin woolen yarn the way Annie did in 1810.

Literary Analysis: The Themes

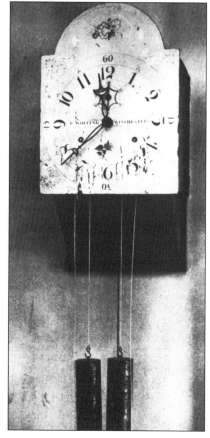

The Clock is about the industrial revolution and its impact on one farm family, but the book is loaded with other well-developed themes. The principal subthemes are: the excesses of materialism; the system of patriarchy and male dominance; and the problem of sexual harassment in the workplace. It is very much a book of the 1980s, when the computer revolution was at the takeoff stage, excesses of greed and materialism of the "yuppie" era were at their high point, and when the women's movement of the 1970s was beginning to have a real impact in the world of work outside the home.

The illustration on page 7 of *The Clock* shows the works of a "tall clock," what we know today as a grandfather clock. (They were too new in 1810 to have been owned by grandfathers.) With a case, they would cost about forty dollars and constitute the most elegant piece of furniture in a middle-class parlor. Some folks, like our (fictional) Mr. Steele would buy the works only for about eight dollars and hang them on a wall to give the weights vertical space to move up and down. Thousands of them were manufactured in Connecticut in the first decades after the 19th century. Our artist copied this one made by Riley Whiting about 1820.

Industrialization

The facts of the introduction of the factory system to New England are described above. Here I mean only to trace that theme as presented in our story. This theme is elucidated for the most part through the clock as symbol of the industrial discipline, contrasted to the descriptions of domestic life lived by "sun time" on a preindustrial farm.

The clock is introduced in the very opening of the story when George described it as "new fangled" (p. 2), a word in current use in 1810; "A marvel. The newest thing," says Pa (p. 6). It takes over the lives of the Steele family—or, at least, Pa tries to make it do so: ". . . he put the whole family on clock time, instead of sun time. The family was supposed to get up by it and eat meals by it, and go to bed by it, never mind if you were hungry or sleepy . . . we couldn't eat until it was six, and the clock allowed us to." (p. 13) "We had our meals to it, said our prayers to it, and went to bed to it." (p. 86) Prayers? Pa worshiped at the clock. He becomes so fixated that on one occasion when Annie returns late from work, bruised, clothes torn, and downcast, "Pa was too busy watching the clock . . . to notice." (p. 99) The family had become prisoners of time. Pa would have put the chickens and cows on an hourly schedule, too, if he could have gotten them to give eggs and milk at the chime of a clock.

In the factory the tyranny of time was even worse. "You had to wait until the bell said you could rest and eat and talk about things. . . . I just had to get used to being hungry when I was told to be hungry." (p. 32) Annie contrasts clock time to sun time when "you could rest a little when you were tired, and take a drink of something when you were thirsty, or a bite of bread and cheese when you were hungry." (p. 32) And finally Annie is punished when she violates the rules of the clock by arriving late at the mill (pp. 40-41). At the mill every worker had to start and stop at exactly the same moment—a moment dictated by the engagement of a great gear connected to the waterwheel that, by a system of belts and shafts, started all the machines at once.

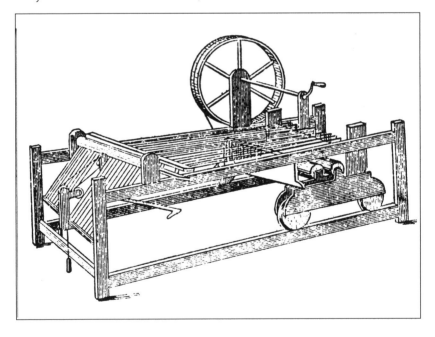

"Now I knew what it meant to work by clock time, instead of sun time," Annie grumbles (p. 32). Even evil was done by the clock: Hoggart conducts his thievery on schedule "regular as clockwork," Tom Thrush explains (pp. 63-64).

The industrial discipline was not only a matter of machine-driven regimentation, but also robotlike repetition, a tedium unbroken by a change of pace, a pause for tea, or even the distractions of conversation—there were rules against that, and anyway, the noise of the machines made conversation impossible. This picture shows a slubbing billy without a holding board at the end with the wheel and a rack of spindles at the other end. Annie would stand by the wheel feeding rolags of wool into the billy that would be drawn out and along the billy to be caught at the far end by hooks and led on to a row of spindles. Though spinning on a wheel at home could be pretty tiresome, at the mill "we didn't march back and forth by the walking wheel; we just stood in one place all day; and that was much more tiresome than all that walking." (p. 30)

By way of contrast, Annie describes the slower-paced—though often tedious—domestic chores. Spinning was dependent on no certain schedule and could always be interrupted for a cup of tea.

Baking, an especially time-driven activity, was still no clock-watcher. You could tell if the oven was hot enough by holding your hand in it and counting. For the rest of it, "Ma could get the timing pretty close on sunny days by watching the sun approach the noonmark . . . on the kitchen windowsill." But "Ma didn't even use the noonmark most of the time—she just knew how much time had passed by natural instinct. . . ." (p. 41), or perhaps rather by generations of tradition and training "the way we always worked before, and our grandpas and grandmas before us and their grandpas and grandmas before them. . . ." (p. 32) The industrial revolution in a couple of generations would overturn centuries of domestic habits.

But the mill brought great benefits along with its regimentation, hazards, and tedium. As Annie knows: "Back on the farm Ma and me would spin all the livelong day half the winter, it seemed like. And if it wasn't spinning it was cutting and sewing. . . . ." (p. 32) And then there was that painful carding (p. 24). The farm work, after all, "was pretty tedious, too, once you'd done it a hundred times." In addition, "Farm work could be cold and wet where the mill was warm and dry; and besides, there was company at the mill." (p. 9). At the mill, at least, "it was nice to be with some girls" (p. 29) rather on the farm where her only friends were pigs and chickens (p. 9). And, of course, as close as the supervision was at the mill, on the farm children hardly ever got away from their parents' eyes. Nor were injuries absent from agricultural work, either. Though the incidence of major harm to the body was certainly greater in factories, Robert, after all, had been disabled on the farm—and would not have died on the wheel if he hadn't first been crippled by a scythe (pp. 15-16, 107).

Pa, of course, is the proselytizer for the new technology. As we've noted, he even had the family pray to the clock (p. 86). "Once only the rich could afford clocks, but with the new methods of manufacturing, these mechanisms will soon be found in every home, no matter how humble," declares Pa, pointing to the democratizing effect of factory-made goods. There will be more jobs and more different kinds of work. "Naturally, demand for clocks will shoot up, and soon there'll be more clockmakers at work than ever. . . . Why it won't be long before home spinning has disappeared," he says presciently. "With machines, the price of cloth has got so, it's hardly worth making your own at home. Someday," Pa continues in words that would have thrilled the hearts of millions of spinsters across the world, "the spinning wheel will be a relic, a reminder of the olden times." (pp. 87-88) Even the girls slubbing away at the billies "can buy all the yarn they need, and have money left over" from their wages (p. 20-21). "And the machine yarn was stronger and smoother than home-spun. . . ." (p. 31).

In the end, Annie asks brother George, "Why did everything have to change?" "Things change, Annie." "Is it better?" Annie asks, posing the question that is the point of our story. George speaks for us when he tells Annie—and our readers, "I don't know, Annie. I guess you'll have to decide that for yourself." (p. 159)

Materialism

There were major advantages to industrializing, no doubt about it. If only it could be kept in balance with other phases of life. This is where Pa became unbalanced. He is the foil for our antimaterialism theme. We know from the start that Pa is addict-ed to *things*—the classic materialist. This characteristic is what leads us to what, for me, is the climactic scene of the book. "Whenever he hears about a new thing he can't rest until he has it," Annie's brother George explains (p. 3)—as if Annie had to be told. Pa's materialism found expression in his concern for money—largely, one supposes, because he could never get enough of it. "Pa liked to talk about money," Annie remarks (p. 16).

So inflamed is Pa about getting things that he willingly sacrifices his son and daughter on the alter of mammon. George spends day after miserable winter day in the woodlot cutting cord after cord for sale. Annie is sent off to the mill, her deeply felt aspiration to be a teacher the price she pays for her father's profligacy. In a most ironic remark, Pa reprimands Annie for objecting to leaving school to go to work in the mill, significantly to earn money to pay his debts, ". . . we can't have everything we want in life." (p. 10)

Our materialist theme is proclaimed at the front of the book in the excerpt from Ralph Waldo Emerson's poem, "Ode Inscribed to W.H. Channing" (1846). Emerson's ode for the most part carries an antislavery theme; he is incensed about the idea of people as chattel, that is, property, things. For our purpose, we quote his antimaterialist lines about how people become the servants of the goods that sustain them. In particular, "Things are in the saddle, / And ride mankind." Pa has an ox, but no horse. He has his eye on one, though, and enthusiastically proclaims his desire: "What we need is a sleigh. Go to church in style and comfort." (p. 70)

Emerson's commentary and Pa's comment set up the thematic climax. Annie, trudging home to the farm on a wintery evening, sees by the light of the rising moon a "creature so strange." This apparition turns out to be her father struggling homeward under a great burden of things: things grotesquely dangling as Pa staggers under the weight of a saddle slung heavily across his back. Things are in the saddle and ride Pa. He has sold his daughter's labor again, and for what? Gewgaws and a saddle when he doesn't even own a horse. He knew he had violated his paternal trust. "He couldn't look at me"; but then when their eyes met, "It was almost like he was begging me to forgive him." But she can't. "He turned, and with the saddle on his back and all those things in the saddle clinking like cowbells, he headed for the house." Annie "stood there watching him go, hating him, hating Mr. Hoggart, hating the mill. . . ." (p. 115) Father's love of material goods is greater than his love for his daughter.

Sexism and Sexual Harassment

Perhaps the most painful self-deception practiced by Pa is his refusal to acknowledge the sexual threat that Hoggart presents to Annie on an almost daily basis. Pa's self-willed refusal to sympathize with his daughter is in part a function of the male-dominated society in which they all live. The patriarchal family structure is taken for granted by everyone. As Ma says, "He's head of this household, and it's his right to do as he likes." (p. 4) "She knew Pa had the right and duty to set the rules around the house," Annie acknowledges (p. 87), but she also questions that "right" when it isn't exercised for the welfare of all: "We shouldn't talk against Pa," George cautions her, "He's our father." Spiritedly, Annie blurts out, "If he's the father, he should have more sense." (p. 26) And Pa's lack of sympathy for his daughter—a lack that has already driven her to confide in someone else's father (pp. 94-96)—alienates her so thoroughly that she finally determines to flee his household to "see if I couldn't make a life for myself that suited me more than the one Pa had planned for me." (p. 125)

Patriarchy was just one part of the male-dominated society Annie, her mother, and all other early 19th-century women lived in. Annie knew that George would get the farm someday, but "Daughters never got anything, unless there were nothing but daughters"; and then in a reference to the prevailing legal concept of *femme sole*—that married women had no legal existence apart from their husbands—she acknowledges "then it would go to their husbands." (p. 2) Even brother George, lovingly sympathetic and protective of Annie, "figured things the same way Pa did—that it wasn't necessary for a girl to study geography and history, when she could be doing something useful to earn her keep." (p. 56)

She was, after all, "just a girl," (p. 124) and though boys could travel the roads alone, no girl could. For girls there was only one future: marriage. Pa alluded to it often enough, and planned for it, but, of course, would be unable to provide a dowry, so Annie would have to "go on working at the mill for years and years, so desperate to get out I'd be willing to marry the first one who asked me." (p. 115)

In this kind of a society, it is no wonder that men felt little compunction about taking advantage of women under their supervision. Our fictional Mr. Hoggart, our research tells us, was not unusual in his cruelty to his youthful workers. His intentions toward Annie are pretty clear from the start, and we hint fairly broadly at what is in store for Annie when she complains on first meeting him, "I didn't like the way Mr. Hoggart looked at me," (p. 28) and later when she reports that Hoggart "crossed his arms and roamed his eyes over me." (p. 37) His pressure gets pretty heavy on a couple of occasions (e.g., p. 46), but he makes it perfectly obvious what he wants when he tells fifteen-year-old Annie, "You're not a girl anymore. You're a woman. You're a woman and can do the things that women do." (p. 79). Recall that we write our books for eighth graders as well as fifth graders, and ten- and thirteen-year-olds will each make of that what they will. Teachers, we assume, need not deal with it at all. At any event, Hoggart's sexual threat is clear enough. It is here that Pa's self-deception is most obvious and most damaging.

Annie is well aware of the gender bias that keeps her in a thoroughly secondary situation. "I'd come to be everybody's toy, for them to play with as they liked. Pa's toy and Mr. Hoggart's toy, and Colonel Humphreys' toy. . . ." (p. 115) By including Humphreys, Annie evinces some awareness of class and the exploitation of labor—especially female labor. But her principal concern is about gender. Pa dismisses Hoggart's sexual advances: ". . . well, you're a pretty girl. These things happen. I suspect he'd been drinking." (p. 98) Even in those days of heavy drinking, Hoggart is known to overindulge (p. 114). One might think that this would deepen Pa's concern for his daughter's safety, chastity, and reputation, but to the contrary, it provides him with an excuse.

It is perfectly obvious what Hoggart is after to everyone, except

Pa. Even when Hoggart explains the deal to Pa—an easy job in the mill in exchange for "behaving well"—Pa refuses to take Annie's complaints seriously. "Now Annie, you've let your imagination run away with you." (p. 114). While he pretends to not believe Annie's account of sexual harassment at the mill, she knows that he does. (p. 84) His self-deception is perfectly clear to her, really. ". . . Pa was bound and determined to believe that going by clock time was a good thing, so he believed it; and he was bound and determined to believe that Mr. Hoggart wasn't really pestering me, either. . . . he saw things the way he wanted them." (p. 55) George agrees. Pa's "near ruined with debt, and he's depending on your wages to keep him going. I think down inside he knows he ought to take you out of the mill. But he can't allow himself to believe that. . . ." (p. 109). Of course, Pa does know what is going on; but he is so desperate for Annie's wages that he closes his mind to reality and continues to live his fantasy of imminent riches.

Annie is trapped in a world made by men, and the only one she has loved has been murdered. Ultimately, however, reality rules, and she has to rely on her brother—not her mother—to protect her at the final crisis. The only difference between Annie and other women in that male-dominated age is that Annie understands and resists her subjugation, while other women did not see or feel beyond the conventions of the time and never expected to rise to an equality with men.

Bibliography

Bagnall, William R. *The Textile Industries of the United States . . . in the Colonial Period.* Cambridge, Mass.: Riverside Press, 1893.
Campbell, Hollis A., William C. Sharpe, and Frank G. Bassett. *Seymour Past and Present.* Seymour, Conn.: W.C. Sharpe, 1902.
Cole, Arthur H. *The American Wool Manufacture.* 2 vols. Cambridge: Harvard University Press, 1926.
Davenport, Elsie G. *Your Handspinning.* Tarzana, Cal.: Select Books, 1964.
Hahn, Stephen, and Jonathan Prude, eds. *The Countryside in the Age of the Capitalist Transformation: Essays in the Social History of Rural America.* Chapel Hill:

University of North Carolina Press, 1985.

Kulik, Gary, and Roger Parks. *The New England Mill Village, 1790-1860.* Cambridge, Mass.: MIT Press, 1982.

Macaulay, David. *Mill.* Boston: Houghton-Mifflin, 1983. This volume with scores of drawings by the author explains and shows how mills of David Humphreys' era were built and worked.

Nylander, Jane C. *Our Own Snug Fireside: Images of the New England Home, 1760-1860.* New Haven: Yale University Press, 1993.

Old Sturbridge Village, in Sturbridge, Massachusetts, is a living museum of all sorts of everyday activities focused on the period 1790-1840. OSV publishes many short works descriptive of the lifestyle portrayed in *The Clock.*

Orcutt, Samuel, and Ambrose Beardsley. *The History of the Old Town of Derby, Connecticut, 1642-1880.* Springfield, Mass.: Springfield Printing Co., 1880.

Prude, Jonathan. *The Coming of Industrial Order: Town and Factory Life in Rural Massachusetts, 1810-1860.* New York: Cambridge University Press, 1983.

Stephens, Ann S. This author published about thirty novels, two of which were laid, at least in part, in Humphreysville in the early nineteenth century: *Bertha's Engagement* (1875) and *The Gold Brick* (1866), as well as her short story, "Malvina Gray."

Play: The Clock

This playlet, adapted by John Rearick for *Scholastic Scope* for noncommercial classroom use was published in March 1994 and is reprinted here with permission. This play condenses the entire book and, of course, gives away the ending. Teachers might want to stage this only after their students have read the book. The play attempts to cover all the themes, but sexual harassment and the exploitation of child labor are the ones that come through clearest.

Characters

Annie Steele, 15-year-old girl
Ma, Annie's mother
Pa, Annie's father
George, her brother
Robert and Hetty, Annie's friends
Tom, an orphan boy

Mr. Hoggart, the overseer
Mr. Brown, Hetty's father
Colonel Humphreys, the mill owner
Narrator, Annie remembering events

SCENE 1

NARRATOR: The trouble started that fall day in 1810 when I came home from school. My brother George was chopping wood near our farm in Connecticut. What worried me was that I didn't see my father.

ANNIE: George, where is Pa?

GEORGE: He's gone to Humphreysville to see the new clock at the store.

ANNIE: Oh, no. He wouldn't buy it, would he?

GEORGE: I sure hope not. I'm already working extra to pay off his debts. But once Pa gets an idea, there's no arguing with him.

ANNIE: Pa's ideas always cost too much. He bought that expensive Merino ram hoping the price of wool would go up. But we are still feeding that ram and he still hasn't gotten any money for it.

NARRATOR: George and I went inside the house to talk to Ma.

MA: Your father can't help himself That's the way he is and you have to accept it.

NARRATOR: Just then we heard Pa coming down the road. He was singing. That was a bad sign. Then he flung open the kitchen door open and stepped inside. He was carrying something.

PA: Wait until you see what I've got. It's the newest thing. A shelf clock.

ANNIE: That's not a whole clock. It's just the gears and insides.

PA: That's the idea. Selling it like this keeps the price down. They turn them out like this in big factories, sell it to you without a case, and the price drops to a mere pittance.

MA: How much did that cost?

PA: Eight dollars.

GEORGE: Eight dollars? I'd have to work a month to earn that!

PA: This clock means progress. From now on we aren't going to be slaves to sun time. We are going to get up, work, and go to bed on clock time.

MA: But Pa, how will you pay for that clock? Shouldn't you pay for the ram first?

PA: I've decided ... I've decided that Annie will work in the mill.

ANNIE: Pa —

PA: That's my decision. It's final.

MA: But Annie wants to stay in school and be a teacher.

PA: It won't be forever, just until I sell the ram and make a profit.

MA: It isn't right. George will inherit the farm some day. But what future will Annie have if she doesn't stay in school?

PA. Annie will just get married. She won't need all that education.

NARRATOR: So, Pa signed the papers. I was to work for six months in Colonel Humphreys's woolen mill—a factory that made wool yarn faster and stronger than we could make it at home. I loved school—just like Ma loved school before she had to leave but now I had to go to work.

SCENE 2

NARRATOR: I knew some people who worked in the mill. My friend Hetty had a job there.

HETTY: Annie, it does get pretty boring. I have to work at the machine 12 hours a day. But farm work gets pretty boring too. And working inside is warmer than being out in the field.

NARRATOR: Robert Bronson, a boy my age, also worked there. He couldn't do farm work because he hurt his foot in an accident. He stayed at the mill but came home to his family on Sunday. I walked home with Robert after church one Sunday and asked him about it.

ROBERT: The mill isn't so bad, Annie. There are new machines and they are bringing in more girls.

ANNIE: Who did the work before the girls?

ROBERT: They got orphan boys from New York, but those boys are hard to control. And Mr. Hoggart, the overseer, is mighty quick to whip them.

ANNIE: What's Mr. Hoggart like?

ROBERT: He's a hard nut. But he's never whipped me. I'm

important. I am the tally boy. I weigh all the wool the farmers bring in.

ANNIE: Would he whip girls?

ROBERT: We never had many girls before now. But it's a fact that he likes to whip people. He hits them mostly for making mistakes and for stealing.

ANNIE: I wouldn't steal anything.

ROBERT: Well, when you come right down to it, Mr. Hoggart is the biggest thief of all. I know that he steals bags of wool because I keep the records.

ANNIE: Shouldn't you tell someone?

ROBERT: Suppose I told someone and they couldn't find any proof. Mr. Hoggart would get even with me. Don't say anything, or I'll get in trouble.

NARRATOR: Robert was my best friend. I knew he was serious about the stealing.

SCENE 3

NARRATOR: The mill was right next to the river because it needed water power to turn the waterwheel. With the sound of the river, the creaking of the waterwheel, and the noisy machines, you had to shout just to be heard. I practically had to yell when Tom Thrush, one of the New York orphans, came around with the lunches.

ANNIE: Tom, what happened to your hand?

TOM: Last year it got caught in one of the machines. I reached in to grab some wool but the machine grabbed me instead.

NARRATOR: Tom was about my age, but he looked much younger. We all looked forward to Tom's coming by. He told us stories about life in New York City and cheered us up. Mr. Hoggart the overseer didn't like him distracting us, though.

HETTY: Tom, you better pray that Mr. Hoggart doesn't catch you talking to us. He'll give it to you good.

TOM: Praying ain't much use to Hoggart. Why, on Sunday he brings us to church, but as soon as the service starts he goes off by himself.

HOGGART: Thrush! Are you bothering the girls again?

NARRATOR: Tom tried to run, but Mr. Hoggart was on him in a flash. He smacked him across the head and knocked him down. He left Tom on the floor.

HOGGART: Annie, I don't want you talking to that boy anymore. He's not good for you.

NARRATOR: When he left, Tom got to his feet.

TOM: I am going to kill Hoggart. The first chance I get I am going to kill him.

SCENE 4

NARRATOR: I was getting used to working at the mill, but it was hard to wake up at 4:30 in the morning when they rang the mill bell. Once I slept late, until 5:30. I was almost two hours late to work.

HOGGART: It's about time you got here. Somebody else had to do your job. You can tell your pa your pay will be a half-day short.

NARRATOR: Pa was counting on my wages. I didn't know what to do. I told Robert.

ROBERT: Your pa is short on money. Maybe you could plead with Mr. Hoggart. He's in the office. I'll wait outside. Shout if there's trouble and I'll come in.

NARRATOR: So I got up my courage and knocked on his door. What do you want?

ANNIE: I promise I'll never be late again if you don't dock my pay.

HOGGART: Oh, it's you.Come on in, Annie, and let's talk about it.

NARRATOR: He shut the door behind me. On the table was a bottle of rum. His breath smelled like strong liquor. Behind him there were open bags of wool.

HOGGART: You know, you are a mighty pretty girl, Annie. I hope that we can be real friendly. I could do a lot for you and make life easy for your friend Robert, too.

NARRATOR: Then he stepped toward me and grabbed my chin so that I had to look right at him. I smelled the liquor on his breath and tried to turn away.

HOGGART: That's not being very friendly.

ANNIE: Please, sir, can I go?

NARRATOR: But he grabbed for me again and tried to kiss me.

Robert opened the door. I could tell Robert was looking at the open bags of wool.

HOGGART: What are you doing here? What are you staring at?

ROBERT: I came to walk Annie home.

NARRATOR: Suddenly, I realized that we had caught Mr. Hoggart stealing wool. He gave Robert a mean look. Did he realize that we knew his secret?

HOGGART: All right, you can go.

SCENE 5

NARRATOR: I told my family how Mr. Hoggart was trying to be "friendly."

ANNIE: He's pestering me.

MA: What do you mean "pestering me"?

ANNIE: He tried to kiss me... and he's stealing wool.

NARRATOR: Pa was staring at me.

PA: Now just a minute, Annie. Let's not jump to conclusions.

GEORGE: If he tries that again, I'll beat the stuffing out of him myself.

PA: I can't believe Mr. Hoggart's that bad. Are you exaggerating this, Annie?

ANNIE: It's true. And that's not all. Mr. Hoggart is stealing wool.

PA: I don't want you to get involved with things like that. It's not your business.

NARRATOR: That was Pa. He was bound and determined to believe that clock time was better than sun time. And he was sure that Mr. Hoggart wasn't pestering me. Without proof, no one would listen to me.

ANNIE: I need to find out where Mr. Hoggart is hiding the wool.

NARRATOR: I tried to talk to Robert about it the next day, but he wasn't weighing the wool, Tom Thrush told me what happened.

TOM: Haven't you heard? Mr. Hoggart has him working a harder job now.

ANNIE: But he can't do that with his injured foot.

TOM: Maybe he can. Maybe he can't. But Hoggart has him carrying big bags of yarn.

ANNIE (*to herself*): He's trying to kill Robert.

SCENE 6

NARRATOR: I got my chance to investigate Mr. Hoggart one snowy evening after church.

MA: Annie, the weather is so bad, why don't you stay over with Hetty's family tonight. They live close to the mill. You won't have to travel back and forth.

ANNIE: Yes, ma.

NARRATOR: Before I went to the Browns' house, I ran back to the mill. I followed a fresh set of footprints in the snow that led to a cabin in the woods. I was careful to step inside the footprints, so no one could tell that I had followed. There was someone in the cabin. I couldn't tell what else was inside. I hid and saw Mr. Hoggart come out. I was pretty sure that the cabin was filled with stolen wool, but I had no way of knowing for sure.

SCENE 7

NARRATOR: A few days later Mr. Hoggart bothered me again. It was time to go home. I was getting my coat on, and suddenly he appeared.

HOGGART: I saw you talking to that dirty little Tom Thrush the other day.

ANNIE: Yes, sir, I might have been talking to him.

HOGGART: I could tell you're not the kind who'd have anything to do with those New York boys. You need a better sort of fellow.

ANNIE: My ma says I'm too young for fellows.

HOGGART: You know, I could make life a lot easier for you and for Robert if you got friendly with me.

ANNIE: Please let me go home.

HOGGART: Better think about what I said.

NARRATOR: When I got home, I told my ma. She said that she'd take care of telling Pa. But I knew that Pa had money troubles to worry about. If I didn't work, he could go to prison for his debts.

SCENE 8
NARRATOR: I had to keep working at the mill. Pa kept talking

about progress and had us all living according to the clock.

PA: The world is changing. Soon there will be machines for everything—for planting and cutting wood. We won't need as many farms. Nobody will have to make their own cloth anymore.

NARRATOR: But nature was still in control of the mill. It got so cold that the waterwheel froze and there was no power. Mr. Hoggart got the boys to knock the ice off the wheel. When it was almost free of ice, Mr. Hoggart stopped and called out.

HOGGART: Send Robert out here.

NARRATOR: Robert came out and I saw Mr. Hoggart tell him to climb on top of the wheel and knock off the last of the ice. Right away I knew what was going to happen: When he chopped away enough ice, Robert would be caught by the wheel as it started to move. I grabbed my coat and ran to the Browns' house.

ANNIE: Mr. Brown, come quick. Mr. Hoggart is going to kill Robert. He has Robert up on the water-wheel. With his bad foot, he won't be able to jump off quickly enough.

MR. BROWN: I don't like the sound of that.

NARRATOR: Mr. Brown ran out of the house with his coat in his hand. I couldn't keep up with him. By the time I got to the mill, Mr. Brown stopped me.

MR. BROWN: You'd better go back, Annie. You don't want to see what happened.

NARRATOR: I ran around him and saw two boys carrying Robert's body away from the wheel. I screamed and Mr. Brown picked me up and carried me away.

SCENE 9

NARRATOR: There was plenty of talk around the village about Robert's death. Some people said it was Mr. Hoggart's fault and others said he wasn't to blame.

PA: Poor Robert, he never had any luck.

ANNIE: It was no accident.

MA: Annie, I don't like Mr. Hoggart, but I can't believe he killed Robert deliberately.

NARRATOR: The worst of it was that I had to go back to the mill. Every time I heard the waterwheel I thought of Robert. I decided to run away if Pa signed me up for another six months of work.

ANNIE *(to herself:)* How am I going to get away? You never see girls alone on the highway. I'll look too suspicious. I'll dress up as a boy and escape to New York.

NARRATOR: When I was coming home from the mill one evening, I saw a strange creature. It had two legs and a big hump on its back. Suddenly I realized that it was Pa carrying a big saddle on his back. We didn't even have a horse!

ANNIE: Pa, you didn't. You wouldn't do that to me. I'll have to go back to the mill for another six month to pay for that!

PA: Annie, I don't want to hear another word. Besides, you got Mr. Hoggart all wrong. I talked to him. He told me that you are a good worker and that he's thinking about giving you an easy job.

ANNIE: Pa, don't you see what he means?

PA: I've made my decision. Everybody has a job to do. Why should you be different?

NARRATOR: I was going to run away. But first I was going to prove Mr. Hoggart was stealing wool and hiding it in that shed.

SCENE 10

NARRATOR: I decided to ask Tom to help me.

ANNIE: Tom, can you keep a secret?

TOM: Yes, Annie, I won't tell a soul.

ANNIE: I am going to run away.

TOM: You mean it? I'll go with you!

ANNIE: I don't know, Tom. I don't want to get you in trouble too.

TOM: Where are you figuring on running to?

ANNIE: New Haven or New York. Do you think we could find work in New York?

TOM: What would you want to work for? You can find enough lying around the dock that you can make off with.

NARRATOR: I decided not to argue. But I could see right away it might be good to have Tom along if I ran away to New York.

ANNIE: But first, Tom, you have to lend me a pair of trousers.

TOM: I could lend them to you, but then I'd have to go naked myself.

ANNIE: You only have one set of clothes?

TOM: Don't worry, Annie, I'll find you some trousers.

ANNIE: And there's one more thing. I want you to help me get into the shed where Mr. Hoggart keeps his stolen wool.

NARRATOR: I told Tom about the shed and he agreed to help me get inside. We worked out a plan. When Ma and Pa were asleep I took a shovel and a pick. I met Tom in a field and we went to the shed together. Under one wall we dug a trench big enough for Tom to climb through.

ANNIE: Tom, can you see what's in there?

TOM: Wool. Bags and bags of it.

ANNIE: How many?

TOM: Annie, I'm no good at counting.

NARRATOR: Tom came out and we covered over the trench. I felt mighty good because I was going to get revenge on Mr. Hoggart. I'd write a letter to Colonel Humphreys, the mill owner.

NARRATOR: I took a piece of paper and carried it to the barn. I used an old barrel as my writing desk.

ANNIE (writing): Dear Colonel Humphreys: Mr. Hoggart has been stealing wool from the mill. He hides it in a little cabin in the woods behind the mill. There is a lot of wool in there now. I saw it. Your friend.

NARRATOR: It was a lie about seeing the wool, but I knew that

Tom had seen it. I took the letter to Colonel Humphreys's house and gave it to his servant. Before I could run away, the servant stopped me and brought me to Colonel Humphreys.

COLONEL HUMPHREYS: Did you write this?

ANNIE: Yes, sir.

HUMPHREYS: Why have you gone to all this trouble to expose Mr. Hoggart?

ANNIE: Because he killed my friend Robert.

HUMPHREYS: That's a very strong accusation.

ANNIE: I know, sir. But it's true.

HUMPHREYS: All right, Annie. You can go along. I'll handle this.

NARRATOR: There was no way of knowing what Colonel Humphreys would do. Maybe he would act like Pa and not do anything. When I got to work the next day I saw that Tom had a black eye.

ANNIE: What happened?

TOM: Somebody saw us coming across the field and told Hoggart.

ANNIE: Tom, we'd better get ready to run away. I'll need those boys' clothes quick as you can get them.

NARRATOR: At the end of the day, as everybody was leaving, I saw Tom walking toward me. He had a hat on his head and walked very stiffly.

TOM: I got those clothes for you.

ANNIE: Where's the package with the clothes?

TOM: What package? I'm wearing two pairs of trousers.

NARRATOR: Just then, Mr. Hoggart appeared. What are you two doing?

TOM: Nothing, sir. We was just talking.

NARRATOR: He knocked Tom over, then he grabbed me.

HOGGART: The servants told me you brought that letter to Colonel Humphreys. Lucky for me, I was able to convince the Colonel that you just liked to stir up trouble. Now, miss, you are going to write another note telling Colonel Humphreys it was all a lie.

NARRATOR: He took out pen and paper.

HOGGART: You write just what I tell you.

NARRATOR: My hand wouldn't move.

ANNIE: I can't write what you want, not after what you did to Robert.

NARRATOR: Hoggart hit me. He pulled his hand back to strike me again, but just then there was a thump. He fell backward, breathing but not moving. Tom was standing behind him with an iron rod.

ANNIE: Don't hit him again, Tom. You'll kill him.

TOM: I aim to.

ANNIE: No!

NARRATOR: Tom and I ran out of the mill. I headed home, but Tom didn't follow.

TOM: No, Annie I am going to go back to New York. Mr. Hoggart is going to beat me, maybe even kill me when he wakes up. If you get to New York, look me up.

SCENE 12
NARRATOR: When I got home, George was cutting wood.

GEORGE: What's the matter, Annie? *(noticing her face)* What happened to you?

ANNIE: Mr. Hoggart hit me and tried to get me to lie about everything.

GEORGE: Take me to that cabin.

NARRATOR: George and I went back through the woods. We saw Mr. Hoggart, a bloody handkerchief tied around his head, at the door of the cabin. He had put a new lock on the door. When he saw me he cursed.

HOGGART: Not you again. Oh, are you in for it.

NARRATOR: But George, who'd spent his life cutting wood, was bigger and stronger. He grabbed Hoggart by the shirt.

GEORGE: Hoggart, I want the key to the shed.

NARRATOR: Hoggart reached into his pocket and pulled out the key. George let Him go and he fell over on his side, like a sack of corn husks. Then we opened the door.

GEORGE: Wool, and plenty of it.

NARRATOR: Hoggart began to crawl away.

ANNIE: Watch out! He's getting away!

GEORGE: It doesn't matter. He's finished around here.

ANNIE: But what happens to me now?

GEORGE: Well, there are Pa's debts to consider. We'd better tell him straight out that unless he works something out we'll leave.

ANNIE: And he'll take back what he's bought?

GEORGE: The saddle anyway. He hasn't got any use for that until we get a horse. But maybe we'd better let him keep the clock. Times are changing. There are going to be more mills. You can't stop progress.

ANNIE: I have to go back to the mill?

GEORGE: You might have to stay there a little longer. And I'll have to keep cutting wood. At least until Pa's debt is whittled down.

NARRATOR: We started off through the woods to Colonel Humphreys's house.

ANNIE: George, why did everything have to change? Why couldn't things stay the same? Now we're just slaves to that clock.

GEORGE: Things change.

ANNIE: Is it better?

GEORGE: I don't know, Annie. You just have to decide that for yourself.

IX. *With Every Drop of Blood*

With Every Drop of Blood is, I believe, the best teaching book of the eight we have published specifically for school use. It is an effort to bring to students some of the complexity of the historiography of the reasons for fighting the Civil War, with particular emphasis on the change in Northern aims from an exclusively constitutional unionism to one that linked union to emancipation. The essay below explains all that, but first let me say a few words about the title.

The Title

The storyline of *Every Drop* follows a series of promises, mostly broken; some fulfilled. The title I had first picked, "And Promises to Keep," was drawn from a line in Robert Frost's "Stopping by the Woods on a Snowy Evening," a poem familiar to many middle schoolers. When I tried out that title on my daughter, a public librarian, it rang a familiar tone and she checked it out on her computer. She found seventeen books with that title. She also thought it was a bit saccharine, too mushy for eleven-year-old boys. I abandoned it, but not before it had found its way into print, and readers will find that title listed in some author directories as one of our books. There is no such book.

Another phantom book results from the necessity of making a copyright deadline for the manuscript before we had agreed on a title. My brother dashed off "Blue and Gray, Black and White," which has a 1992 copyright, but no book. The only published version is the one called *With Every Drop of Blood.*

This title came after I considered and rejected "Bloody

Promises," and read around a bit searching for something appropriate. I found it in Lincoln's second inaugural address of March 4, 1865, forty days before the president's assassination. An excerpt from that address is printed at the front of the book. It seemed so rhetorically symmetrical to me that I set it up as lines in a poem. That is not the way Lincoln wrote it. The lines of particular relevance to our title proclaim that the war will continue "until every drop of blood drawn with the lash shall be paid by another drawn with the sword."

It is widely reported that when Lincoln met Harriet Beecher Stowe on December 2, 1862, he said, "So this is the little lady who started this big war." Beyond family tradition reported years later by Stowe's children, there is no evidence that he actually said that or anything like it. But it is a virtual certainty that Lincoln had read *Uncle Tom's Cabin* some time during the decade after its publication. It is interesting that in that book, Stowe has the morbidly heartless overseer, Simon Legree, in the course of giving Tom a fatal flogging, holler, "I'll count every drop of blood there is in you, and take 'em one-by-one, till ye give up." And a little later, Legree says again—just as Tom forgives him and dies, "I'll take every drop of blood he has, unless he confesses." (pp. 582, 584 in Penguin Classics edition, 1986) These were exactly the drops of "blood drawn with the lash" that Lincoln alluded to in his address.

Historiography

This book is not so much about the causes of the Civil War as it is about the reasons why men fought in it. The causes of the war were multiple, of course, and the debate among professional historians revolves around variable emphases. There is no "single causist" among them, though there has been a strong consensus over the past generation that the principal cause had to do with slavery. Historiographically, interpretations of the causes of the war have, as is to be expected, reflected the larger intellectual and economic contexts of their times.

During the Reconstruction Era right after the war, Northern historians saw the conflict as a moral crusade to end the evil of slavery. Southerners continued to justify it as a constitutional argument over states' rights and the nature of federalism, an interpretation that enjoyed a national consensus at the opening of the War. Until 1863, Lincoln consistently insisted that the maintenance of the Union was all he had in mind.

The Progressive Era with its focus on economics, and the Depression of the 1930s again made economic matters foremost in everyone's mind. Many historians were brought to the belief that economic concerns such as tariff and railroad policy, the opposition of free labor to slave labor, and the international implications of the cotton trade were the root cause of the division of 1861 (p. 24). Other historians pointed to a "conflict of cultures," of Puritan and Cavalier, of factory hand and farmhand, free labor and slave labor. Yet another variation emphasized the failure of blundering politicians and irresponsible agitators. Opposed to those were historians who saw the war as an irrepressible conflict over the moral questions surrounding the institution of slavery. Both sides in the 1850s and 1860s brought biblical injunction to support their cause.

This brief review greatly simplifies the very complicated and complex interpretations of professional historians writing over the past century and a quarter. But I trust that it does help to convey some sense of that complexity. There are numerous works for interested teachers to consult in order to get a firmer grasp on these historiographic debates. Perhaps the most convenient, though a bit dated, is the compilation by Kenneth M. Stampp listed in the bibliography below. Here I intend only to point to places in *With Every Drop of Blood* that reflect these different interpretations and offer an opportunity for teachers to explore them with their students.

Johnny poses the question early on when first confronted with the possibility of his father's death: "That was when I began to wonder what the war was for." (p. 18) He had not wondered earlier because Pa seemed clear about it. Pa "didn't think twice" about enlisting. It was going to be a short war and "he was defending his own people—his own family, when you got down to it." (p. 4) But as the war continued for month after bloody month and finally years, Johnny, Pa, and the rest of the Southern Confederacy needed a broader-scale justification. The war was a matter of constitutional rights, Pa explains. "The U.S. Constitution says each state is equal . . . this here war isn't about slaves at all—it's about a state's right to govern itself." (p. 29)

The principal basis for this claim is the historical one that the states existed before the United States and it was their creation. That was made clear, so says Pa, by the addition of the Tenth Amendment to the Constitution that restricted the powers of the national government (p. 30). That amendment says, "The powers not delegated to the United States by the Constitution, nor prohibited by it to the States, are reserved to the States respectively, or to the people." The counter to this argument is voiced by the Yankee Captain Bartlett. The Constitution, he points out, "starts off with the words, 'We the people of the United States', not 'We the states.' You can't have every state that disagrees with the laws thumbing its nose at the national government and going off by itself." (p. 150) This was directly opposed to Pa's insistence that "the states weren't beholden to the Federal government, that they're free and independent." (p. 30)

It is one of the ironic truisms of the Civil War that both sides justified their actions on constitutional grounds. Similarly, both sides appealed to the Declaration of Independence to support their positions. The Declaration, Johnny explains to Cush, was "the most important thing that ever was. It's when we declared we was free of the British, and fought the Revolution over it. Same as the South declared it was free of the Federal government." (p. 115) The states' rights dispute gets its most passionate play when Johnny insists, "The Constitution says plain as day that the union was put together by the states and could be pulled apart by the states. Virginia had a right to quit, and the Federals didn't have no business coming down on us the way they did." (p. 94) But Cush juxtaposes the Bible to the Constitution: "States' rights ain't got nothing to do with it. The war's about some people bein' held in bondage by other people. It's in the Bible. 'Ye are all children of God by faith in Christ Jesus.' We all the same in His eyes and no one should be set over another." (pp. 94-95). Constitutional and moral justification of the war are contrasted here.

At first Johnny accepted Pa's basic justification of the war as a constitutional struggle. But Pa's explanation was muddled. Pa was not fighting to protect slavery—he owned no slaves and "didn't go out there and get myself shot over a passel of nigras. That wasn't the point of fighting." (p. 28) But, he adds, Virginians can't "let the Federals take away our slaves. . . ." (p. 29) And to further confuse the issue, Pa finally has to admit, "Whatever else there is to it, a man who took any pride in his Southern honor couldn't sit still" for Northerners trying to take over (p. 32).

But then, around the teamsters' campfire, Johnny gets an earful of a different view. "Well, I don't know about states' rights," says the doomed Jeb Wagner. "What I won't stand for is having a nigger put up as good as a white man." Jeb, we can be sure, owned no slaves, so it was important to him that he hold status some other way, and that was in racial superiority, the cement of the white South. "Yessir," he concludes, "I'm for states' right, all right—states' rights to keep their slaves." (p. 64) Racism was not confined to Southerners, however. Pa tells Johnny that "a lot of them very Yanks that are down here getting themselves shot to pieces don't want nigras around any more than I do." (p. 31)

And Johnny knows about the New York City draft riots in which working-class whites—mostly immigrant Irishmen—beat Negroes, burned their homes and a church and finally lynched a half dozen of them. When twenty thousand troops were brought in to quell the four-day riot, casualties rose to about a thousand.

It was the worst race riot—indeed the worst riot—the United States has ever seen. And it happened in the North. Johnny knew about this; racism was a national curse. (pp. 137-38) One of the black soldiers has to agree, "It ain't heaven up there . . ." (p. 138). By this time Johnny is thoroughly confused about why the war is being fought. "It seemed like a lot of people were fighting the Yanks just because they were here." (p. 64)

Johnny couldn't let the question rest. For what had his father died? "If the war wasn't about slavery, what was it about? States' rights, sure—I didn't want the Yankees pushing us around anymore than anybody did. But states' rights to do *what*? The whole thing had me mighty confused." (p. 184) Maybe, Johnny finally ponders, the war was really about black and white folks being equal, but "Blame me if I was sure." (p. 229)

Literary Analysis

Though we like to leave a lot of questions dangling for readers to try to get a grip on, we do take a position in *With Every Drop of Blood*. That is, that the war *became* one in which the original official Union objective to prevent secession—a constitutionally based stance—was linked inseparably to emancipation and the end of slavery. This is certainly the prevailing consensus among professional historians as I write now at the end of the 20th century. In *Every Drop* we make the point over and over.

The beginning of a policy of emancipation came with congressional legislation in March 1862 forbidding army officers from returning runaway slaves. This act gave rise to the idea of treating slaves the same as any other enemy property, that is as contraband goods. Slaves freed this way were referred to as contrabands, as Johnny explains (p. 41). That slavery as a cause could not be avoided becomes clear as Pa tries to reject it; he can't explain states' rights except in the context of slavery (p. 29). But Cush sees it the other way, "States' rights ain't got nothing to do with it," (p. 94) he says, separating Lincoln's initial profession from the objective Lincoln joined with it later.

At this point, Cush provides a biblical justification for racial equality. Americans of the 19th century were a profoundly religious people. Johnny and Cush are typical in their biblical knowledge and faith in the Bible's authority. For Americans everywhere, the Bible was an ultimate source. Indeed, *Uncle Tom's Cabin* was written to show that slavery was not compatible with Christianity. That tract was necessary because in the debate over slavery in the antebellum era, the proslavery side had the best of biblical support. It may be shocking to the modern mind that this is so, but it is clear that the Old Testament approves slavery as a God-given social institution, and the New Testament nowhere condemns it; slavery was an accepted practice at the time of Christ's presence on Earth—and for centuries after. There are many references in the Old Testament to mankind as property—purchased, gained in war, or as a punishment for moral and legal crimes.

The episode that formed the bedrock of biblical justification of slavery among the general public was that described in Genesis 9:26, and which is the subject of discussion among the Southern teamsters (pp. 62-63) and the basis of Johnny's argument, "Well what about Genesis where it says, 'Cursed be Canaan; a servant of servants shall he be unto his brethren.' It's clear enough—God made the colored black so's they could be told apart from whites." (p. 141) This is a pretty succinct but accurate state of folk wisdom of the time. Johnny is giving the generally accepted version of the story of Ham's shame in viewing his father, Noah, lying naked in a drunken stupor. Ham's brothers cover Noah, but Noah places the curse of perpetual slavery on Ham's son Canaan and his descendants unending. Canaan's brothers, Cush, Mizrah, and Put, were excused. Since Canaan's kingdom was between the Jordan River and the Mediterranean, by some extension of African characteristics, Canaan's descendants were further cursed with black skins. Confused with this story in the public mind—even the educated public—was the story of Cain and Abel in Genesis 4. As a punishment for killing his brother Abel, Cain is doomed by God to life as a vagabond and fugitive. This is too much for Cain to take: He cries, "it shall come to pass, that everyone that findeth me, shall slay me." The Lord forbade the murder of Cain and "set a mark upon Cain, least any finding him, should kill him." (Genesis 4:14-15) Apparently in the popular mind Cain and Canaan became conflated, and Cain's mark also became the curse of blackness. This is the confused version presented by the teamsters and disputed by Johnny (pp. 62-63).

On the other side, the Bible provides little support for Cush's antislavery position. The best case is made by drawing support from the general spirit of love and charity that informs much of the New Testament. Cush points out that all Christians are equally children of God, for instance (p. 95). He is willing to accept Johnny's fraudulent reading of the Gettysburg Address, "All men are created eagles," because he knows the verse from Isaiah, "They that wait upon the Lord renew their strength; they shall mount up with wings as eagles; they shall run, and not be weary." (40:31). And it comes with little grace for Cush to be told by Johnny, "Servants, be obedient to them that are your masters," (Ephesians 6:5), when Johnny has jeopardized his life and his family's welfare because he did not obey the voice of his father.

The thematic spine of *With Every Drop of Blood* is the intellectual journey that carries Johnny from accepting black chattel slavery as part of both the natural and divine universe to at least a willingness to consider the proposition that all men are created equal (p. 228).

This theme is played out around Johnny's effort to understand the meaning of his father's death. What was the war all about? The idea that it was about slavery is introduced and rejected in Pa's effort to explain the war in terms of states' rights and honor. But he isn't very convincing (pp. 28-29). Cush brings the emancipationist interpretation directly to him when, for the first time, Johnny is forced to confront the black perception: "Pretty soon the North is going to be master of the South, and us colored is going to have you buckras steppin' mighty lively." (p. 95) The day of jubilee, says Cush, alluding to that day every fifty years when servants shall be released (Leviticus 25 and 26). Johnny's unruly feelings were held in check at this declaration only because Cush was pointing a rifle at his head. But Johnny gradually comes around.

Johnny's conversion to the equalitarian understanding of the meaning of the war parallels Lincoln's public stance. The president insisted from the start that the only aim of his government was to maintain the Union. Well into the war, he still protested that if he had to free some, all, or none of the slaves in order to preserve the Union, he would do it. The Gettysburg Address is Lincoln's official public admission that the war aims had been augmented in a fundamental way. There were now two equally important objectives inseparably linked—union *and* emancipation.

At first Johnny knows that it is beneath the dignity of white men to have to fight black men as equals (p. 76). Darkies, after all, "weren't smart enough for much," (p. 77) and "even the Yankees had enough sense to realize you needed white people to tell the darkies what to do." (p. 81) But Johnny sees so much intelligence in Cush that he decides Cush must be different from all the other blacks (p. 105). Indeed, Johnny is surprised when Cush takes offense at his slighting remarks about Cush's father. "Of course, I wouldn't like it, neither, if somebody said my pa deserved a whipping, but I didn't expect Private Turner to feel the same as me." (p. 108) Some light begins to open Johnny's mind as he recognizes the thirst for learning and the quick intelligence of Cush. We make this point by having both Pa and Cush use the same analogy to describe the price for growing up ignorant: spending the rest of your life "looking at the wrong end of a mule," (p. 26 and 109), a point Cush made earlier: "I'm gonna get some learning and kiss that old plow good-bye for good." (p. 99)

Johnny, while trying to absorb the idea that Cush is smart

enough to learn his ABCs while lying in the dirt under the schoolhouse floor, he also disparages superstitions about snakes as a characteristic of ignorant blacks. He adds, however, that even he believed "that sometimes they were true," (p. 106) and later Johnny evinces his own superstitious self when he blanches at the idea of stealing clothes off a dead man: "Aren't you afraid you'll get haunted afterward?" (p. 181)

However, Johnny is in the parlance of our own day, a screwup. He got himself into this near-fatal mess by violating his word to his father, discounting the known risks of the expedition, and lying to his mother. He knows he's a fool who acts before he thinks. His mother has told him so often enough (p. 6, quoting Proverbs 14:129), and he chastises himself often, as well. "What a blame fool I was," he thinks when he finds himself in the middle of his first battle, (p. 71) and when he is captured he is "sick and ashamed. . . ." (p. 75) When Cush points out how dangerous it was for Johnny to put on a Union uniform, Johnny has to admit "I felt like a fool, all right." (p. 159) And more than that, "I could see, Cush was right."

Indeed, even earlier Johnny had begun to notice that Cush was not so dumb. It is true that neither boy knew what the capital of South Carolina was (pp. 93-94. It was moved from Charleston to Columbia in the 1790s). But Johnny, who once "found it hard to believe that there was a darky in the world that had any brains," learned that Cush "was going to be harder to fool than I reckoned on. . . ." (p. 110, 111) As Johnny digs the boys deeper and deeper into trouble, he has to admit "It's all my fault," and rely on Cush to talk their way out of it (p. 173).

Of course, Cush, too, had his shortcomings. He let his emotions lead him astray when sympathy for Johnny and his own desire to keep up the reading lessons cause him to slight his guard-keeping duties. Cush cannot escape complicity in getting the boys into the troubles that came close to killing them both.

As Johnny is humbled by his repeated errors in judgement and his tendency to act without thinking, he also begins to see that there are different perspectives on matters he has been brought up to believe are settled. Reflecting his slaveless father's views, he thinks, "People said most masters would be a sight better off without slaves, but only allowed them to stay out of kindness, for darkies didn't have the brains to take care of themselves, if they was turned lose. But I could see now that was only one side to it. I never asked a darky how they felt about being slaves." (p. 142) "Up there on High Top Mountain," Johnny ruminates, "the mules were more important to us than darkies. But now I'd gotten to know a darky, and I could see it wasn't simple. It made my head ache." (p. 145)

After ten days of close living and mutual support under combat conditions, Johnny notes that Cush "couldn't think of me as the enemy any more." Of course, we put Johnny in a Union uniform, not only for purposes of plot (as a matter of fact, it complicated the plot somewhat) but as a symbolic suggestion of sameness. And the boys were not only dressed the same but they were the same under the skin. Both had lost fathers; both wanted more than anything to get back to their mothers (pp. 182, 145, 184). And both boys pass supreme tests of friendship, risking their lives to save the other (pp. 153-4, 176, 184). They had "got to be friends by mistake," Johnny muses, and Cush agrees, "kind of took me by surprise, too." (pp. 176 and 226)

Johnny's real epiphany comes while the boys are fleeing both Union and Confederate troops—all because of a whole series of Johnny's missteps that have implicated Cush, too. At first Johnny articulates his new wisdom as an answer—an unwanted answer—to the question of why his father had to die.

If the war wasn't about slavery, what was it about? States' right, sure—I didn't want the Yankees pushing us around anymore than anybody did. But states' rights to do *what*? The whole thing had me mighty confused. I sure didn't want to see Cush going back to his old master and get whipped whenever the master felt like it, for I could see he wouldn't like getting whipped any more'n I did. And if it wasn't right for Cush to be whipped regular, why was it right for any of them to get whipped? (p. 184)

As the boys start back to their homes—both in the Shenandoah Valley—to return to their mothers, the wagon and mules still intact, Johnny says, "I tell you what, Cush. If you was to ride on Regis, and I was to sit in the wagon, it'd set better with folks along the way." (p. 227)

> He gave me along look. "That ain't much of an improvement over the way things was, Johnny."
> "We got to give it time, Cush."
> "What's the war for, then?"
> I sat there thinking. All along that'd been the hardest nut to crack. Pa said it was states' rights, Captain Bartlett said it was to keep the Union together, Jeb Wagner said it was to keep the darkies in their place, Cush said it was to free them. And what was it Lincoln promised in that blame speech of his? "Our forefathers brought forth a new nation dedicated to the proposition that all men are created equal"? Pa never believed blacks were the equal of whites, and Ma didn't, neither, I reckoned, except maybe in the eyes of God—their souls were just as likely to rise up to Heaven as white folks. But Lincoln, he believed it, and I reckoned a lot of folks in the North believed it, too. So maybe that was what the fighting was for, after all. "All men are created equal," I said. "Do you suppose that's it?"
> "Got to be," Cush said. "It's what the Declaration promised, wasn't it?" (p. 228)

If Johnny wasn't smart, maybe he was wise, or at least fundamentally right-hearted. Eventually, we show Johnny's errors to be those of heart over mind. He puts himself in great danger to save Cush a couple of times, and on one of those occasions, he says that if he "had any brains at all," he'd leave the wounded Cush to shift for himself. "But seeing as I haven't got the sense I was born with, I reckon I better cart you along in the wagon until your leg gets healed up some." (p. 185) Down deep, Johnny had friendly feelings for Cush early on. Almost at their first encounter he refrains from calling him a nigger (p. 99) and figured "it would only be Christian" to tone down his denigrating language (p. 108). Soon, Johnny begins to think,

> Blame me if he didn't think we were already friends. We hadn't been riding along together but three days. I guess it came from rambling along about how he learned his *ABC's* and what kind of church we went to. To tell the truth, I wouldn't have minded having a friend right then. When you got down to it, he was a nice enough fella, willing to talk about things. And if he'd been white and on our side, I'd have jumped at the chance to make friends with him. To be honest, I'd have jumped at it even if he wasn't on our side. But I just couldn't bring myself to do that with a darky. Oh, I didn't mind being *friendly* with Cush, and rambling on about things, but that wasn't the same as being real friends. (p. 127).

This was after three days together. By the time another week went by, they were risking their lives to save each other. And Johnny has to admit that, at least in Lincoln's eyes, the war was being fought to bring about the day—Cush's jubilee—when "All men are created equal." (p. 192) Johnny's fellow Rebs were still determined never to sit down to eat with a black man (p. 62), and though Johnny's mother might give Cush some biscuits and gravy, "he'd have to sit there on the woodpile and eat while the white folks sat inside." (p. 227) And Johnny had to agree "it is going to be a long time before kids of slaves and kids of slave owners will be able to sit at the table of brotherhood," a paraphrase of the closing words of Martin Luther King's "I Have a Dream" speech of

August 28, 1963. But, Johnny goes on to ask, "Could we still be friends? I didn't know. But I figured I'd try. 'Well, Cush, you can walk home if you like, just to let everybody know you're free. But if it was me, I'd ride that mule. It's a sight more pleasant to have some company along the way.' He nodded. 'There's something to that, Johnny.'" (p. 229)

The Battles

The literature of the Civil War is immense. Over a hundred thousand books have been published on the subject in English alone. It is an event that never ceases to attract scholarly and popular attention. There are scores of excellent works about the battles, most of them replete with maps and illustrations, a few of which are listed in the bibliography below. My effort here is a very modest one, to provide only enough information to put the battles that figure in *With Every Drop of Blood* in a comprehensible chronological, geographic, and strategic context.

As the maps in the front of *With Every Drop of Blood* show, Johnny Miller lives in the Shenandoah Valley, in Rockingham County, a place of scattered villages and towns with a population in 1860 of about twenty thousand of which a bit over 10 percent were black—almost all of whom were slaves. This is a much smaller proportion than for Virginia as a whole; in neighboring Madison County to the east, for instance, over 50 percent of the whole population were slaves. Rockingham County was not far from the mountainous region that refused to secede when Virginia did and became the state of West Virginia in 1863. The valley had been settled in the late 18th century by a large contingent of Germans. We have given the local folks German-sounding names. Our family is the Millers, but that is not made known in the book. The Reamer mill and Conrad's store are historical realities.

The Shenandoah Valley was a rich breadbasket, important for

providing wheat, corn, and pork to the rest of Virginia, where so much of the farmland was devoted to cash crops like tobacco. It was also an entry route to Washington, and thus a much fought over region. Harpers Ferry sits at the confluence of the Shenandoah and the Potomac. In the early years of the war Stonewall Jackson's Rebel troops dominated the area and kept it safe for the local farmers. Indeed, the war once came very close to Johnny's home in 1862, when Stonewall Jackson drove the Union troops out of the valley. Later, however, as the tide began to turn in favor of the Union, the devastation of the valley became part of the effort to starve the Confederacy into submission. The dashing Philip Sheridan was ordered to destroy everything that might help sustain the Southern war effort. He did his job well, and by late 1862 the valley was a scene of desolation, blackened fields, battered woodlots, burned buildings, and broken families.

The Union raid in which the Millers' provisions were stolen (pp. 5-6) would have been part of Sheridan's campaign, possibly an offshoot of his raid on Winchester in September 1864. The Battle of Cedar Creek, where Pa was wounded, took place on October 19, 1864, and after an initial victory by Confederate forces, Sheridan rallied his men and routed the Rebels. This battle brought the Shenandoah campaign to a virtual end with the Union forces now dominant.

The Valley Campaign was one of the most bitter of the war, not only because of the destruction of civilians' property, but also because of the character of the fighting. Sheridan was constantly harassed by local guerrillas, who shot stragglers, burned wagon trains, and disappeared into the woods. Since they often fought in civilian clothes, Yankee soldiers hung captured guerrillas; and the guerrillas retaliated in like manner. The most effective of the guerrilla leaders was Colonel John S. Mosby. His troops, Mosby's Raiders, became the scourge of Union forces all the way from the valley to Richmond, fifty miles away.

On a scale of bitterness, however, nothing could match the results of the Fort Pillow "Massacre" of April 12, 1864 (p. 70).

Here, on the Mississippi River in Tennessee, a force of 262 black and 295 white Union soldiers were overrun after refusing to surrender to about three times their number of Confederates. Though Northern and Southern accounts differ, the best most recent scholarly writing supports the Northern claim that Southern troops massacred the black soldiers after they had surrendered, burying some alive and setting afire the tents of the wounded. Black soldiers, who were just beginning to see action in large numbers, never forgot this incident.

The centerpiece of our story is the Siege of Petersburg. This was a campaign extending from June 1864 to April 1865. The effort, of course, was to capture Richmond, the Confederate capital. By the summer of 1864 Robert E. Lee had concentrated most of his forces in the Richmond area. Petersburg, about twelve miles south of Richmond, was the railroad hub of all but one of the lines to Richmond. If Petersburg could be taken, and the one remaining railroad line to the west destroyed, Lee would be bottled up. He could not hold out long under those circumstances. In June he moved the main body of his troops to Petersburg.

Efforts to take Petersburg by frontal assault failed in June and Grant was forced to settle in for a long-term siege. Both sides dug massive systems of trenches and abutments of logs and spikes. Six weeks of blazing dry heat was followed by too much rain. Both sides kept up mortar fire, sometimes simultaneously in duels, more often randomly. Sharpshooters took a constant toll. Patrols feeling for weak spots met and fought. In all, about forty-two thousand Union and twenty-eight thousand Confederate troops were killed, wounded, or captured, during the siege.

The Union forces controlled City Point, a dock and railroad rendezvous, the entrepôt for vast stores of supplies that kept the bluecoated soldiers well fed, well clothed, and well doctored. Meanwhile civilians and soldiers in Petersburg and Richmond, supplied only by the one rail line coming from the west and the few wagon trails of blockade-runners that managed to get through, were short of everything and reduced to eating their dogs. Finally, Lee decided he had to make one last desperate effort to break out. This he did on the night of April 2 and Grant ordered a general assault at 4:30 the next morning. Thus began the parallel movement of both forces westward, with continuous fighting all the way to Appomattox.

Johnny and Cush, with their mules and wagon, are attempting to go northwest up to the Shenandoah Valley (p. 186). They can go west, but every time they turn north they find themselves in the middle of the fighting. They just "couldn't get shet of the war," Johnny explains (p. 188). The list of villages and crossings along the way (p. 188) is in fact a list of places where small battles or skirmishes took place. This picture shows a mule train like the one Johnny traveled with. Here it is crossing the Rappahannock River on a pontoon bridge like the one Johnny crosses to get over the James River to City Point—a very much longer bridge.

From Petersburg to Appomattox is about a hundred miles by road; perhaps seventy-five as the crow flies, as we show on the map in the front of the book. Johnny and Cush left Petersburg on April 1 during the Union bombardment that forced Lee's flight that morning. The boys had traveled "three or four days" by page 187, and must have spent three more on the road before Cush's capture on April 8. The next day brought Lee's surrender in Major Wilmer McLean's house at the village of Appomattox courthouse. The peaceful conclusion of the book, we assume, comes as no surprise to our readers. It is foreshadowed in the croaking of the infant frogs that peep so poignantly for Johnny (p. 213), but my guess is that readers knew that the war ended at Appomattox even before they began the book. If not, perhaps they will be pleasantly surprised.

Bibliography

There are well over a hundred thousand works of nonfiction about the Civil War. The list here represents only a few of the most recent publications I found useful in writing *With Every Drop of Blood*.

Castle, Henry A. *The Army Mule and Other War Sketches.* Indianapolis: Bowen-Merrill Co., 1897

Collier, Christopher and James L. Collier. *The Civil War.* Tarrytown, N.Y.: Marshall Cavendish, 1999.

Cornish, Dudley Taylor. *The Sable Arm: Black Troops in the Union Army, 1861-1865.* Lawrence: University Press of Kansas, 1987 [1956].

Cullen, Joseph P. *The Siege of Petersburg.* Conshohocken, Penna.: Eastern Acorn Press, 1981 [1970].

Davis, David Brion. *The Problem of Slavery in the Age of Revolution, 1770-1823.* Ithaca, N.Y.: Cornell University Press, 1975. The last chapter discusses the use of the Bible to justify slavery.

Griffith, Paddy. *Battle Tactics of the Civil War.* New Haven: Yale University Press, 1989.

Hess, Earl J. *The Union Soldier in Battle.* Lawrence: University Press of Kansas, 1997.

Higginson, Thomas Wentworth. *Army Life in a Black Regiment.* New York: Collier Books, 1962 [1870].

Lamb, Robert Byron. *The Mule in Southern Agriculture.* Berkley: University of Southern California Press, 1963.

McPherson, James M. *Battle Cry of Freedom: The Civil War Era.* New York: Oxford University Press, 1988.

Moseman, C.M. *Moseman's Illustrated Catalog of Horse Furnishing Goods.* New York: Dover Publications, 1987 [1893].

Pond, George E. *The Shenandoah Valley in 1864.* New York: Charles Scribner's Sons, 1883.

Robertson, James I. *Civil War Virginia: Battleground for a Nation.* Charlottesville: University Press of Virginia, 1991.

Stampp, Kenneth M. *The Causes of the Civil War.* New York: Simon and Schuster, 1991 [1959].

Stern, Philip Van Doren. *Soldier Life in the Union and Confederate Armies.* Bloomington: Indiana University Press, 1961.

Time-Life Books, *The Battle Atlas of the Civil War.* New York: Barnes and Noble, 1996. Originally, *Echoes of Glory,* 1991.

Wayland, John W. *History of Rockingham County, Virginia.* Dayton, VA: n. pub., 1912.

Wheeler, Richard. *Witness to Appomattox.* New York: Harper Collins, 1989.

Wiley, Bell I. *The Common Soldier of the Civil War.* New York: Charles Scribner's Sons, 1973.

Williams, George F. *Bullet and Shell: The Civil War as the Soldier Saw It.* Stamford, Conn.: Longmeadow Press, 1992 [1884].

X. *Censored: An Author's Perspective*

Twelve-year-old Timmy Meeker, struggling with his brother's seventeen-year-old girlfriend over an incriminating piece of paper, slammed her as hard as he could on the side of her head. "You little bastard," shouts Betsy (p. 84). This is a line my brother wrote for one of the climactic moments in *My Brother Sam Is Dead.* Can it be that all across America ten-year-old girls are sitting in fifth-grade classrooms reading out loud "You little bastard" to their classmates? Judging from the reaction from outraged parents, one would think so. But I doubt it. I haven't yet met a teacher of any experience who would set things up that way. Nevertheless, the use of *Brother Sam* in classrooms across the country is challenged scores of times every year. In 1996 People for the American Way listed it among America's ten most challenged books—just after Steinbeck's *Of Mice and Men.*

The use of profanity and obscenity was not the only reason for the challenge, however. Parents complained about graphic descriptions of battlefield scenes, the consumption of alcohol, and an "unpatriotic" view of the American Revolution. At one large protest meeting, which I attended unrecognized, one woman objected to the book because one of the authors once wrote for *Playboy* (which is true—but it wasn't me). Although the board of education in this last instance decided to keep the book in the library, often enough the decision is the reverse.

We write these books primarily to teach American history. The bottom line is that students will learn nothing from them unless they read them. They won't read them—and if they do they won't remember what they read—unless the story engages, interests, and excites them. For that to happen we must reach our readers on an emotional level. The scenes we draw must have impact: that means not only intellectual engagement with the ideas we present, but also emotional engagement with the characters we depict. Indeed, though history itself holds unending materials for dramatic narrative, it is difficult to capture the actual emotional content of historical figures' characters. It is a lot more honest and literarily feasible to use fictional characters to personify and imbue with emotion the ideas we want kids to understand and remember. Thus strongly connotative, colorful, and striking words are a major literary tool to create character, context, and their interrelationships, all to bring about real historical understanding.

Dealing with censorship is not new to me. My first encounter with attempts to bar books from classroom use came when I, a new untenured teacher of eighth graders, had a panel of six high-level students read and discuss George Orwell's *1984*. This was in the mid-1950s, Joe McCarthy's heyday. They were spooky times. It was on this occasion that I learned the first of the Six Lessons about Censors that I describe here.

Lesson One. The censors have not read the book.

When one of my eighth graders carried home a paperback copy of *1984* with a slightly lurid cover—for 1955—depicting a bosomy young woman wearing a sash across which was emblazoned "Anti-Sex League," my principal heard from my student's mother. To his lasting credit and my lasting gratitude, the principal permitted me to meet in his office with the horrified parent, who also happened to be the reigning president of the PTA. I asked her what she objected to. I was degrading her daughter's taste by giving her communist—remember the era—trash. But what was it in the book that was communist or degrading, I was allowed to persist. I wouldn't read this garbage, said Mrs. PTA.—and she hadn't. Nevertheless, I was told to remove the book from my course, and asked to submit all my future reading lists to the principal. How to squelch young enthusiasm for innovation and excitement in the classroom.

Another episode illustrating Lesson One—censors have not

read the book—is much more recent: 1993, in fact. *Jump Ship to Freedom* follows the risky adventures of a young slave who gets mixed up in the writing of the U.S. Constitution in 1787. In the course of the year or so the book covers, Daniel Arabus rejects his view of himself as a stupid nigger and comes to see that he is as brave, smart, honest, and wise as any white person he meets. He grows from ". . . I was black and wasn't as smart as white folks," (p. 2) to "it seems to me that there ain't much difference one way or another . . . . take the skin off of us, and it would be pretty hard to tell which was the white ones and which ones wasn't." (p. 187) A pretty uplifting story, it seems to me. Although readers encounter the word darky as early as page 11, it is not until page 20 that they smash into nigger. One black sixth grader never got past page 2 before complaining to his teacher. The school principal pulled the book from the library shelves; a little tempest brewed and local NAACP officials became involved. In the end, *Jump Ship* was removed from elementary but not middle-school library shelves, though the teachers "all agreed not to use the book in lessons so as not to offend students."

The fracas generated some interesting comment. "Parents argued," a newspaper account explained, "that the book was dangerous because some students will only flip through the beginning of the book and not read it all." This view raises an intriguing question: Must all books for school use be written so that no single page if read alone will not offend anyone? There is no evidence that any of those objecting to the book ever read it; indeed their comments lead pretty clearly to the conclusion that they did not. I will return to "the N word" later.

Lesson Number Two: Censors are mindless. We often run into situation where editors of anthologized excerpts from our books want to remove words, phrases, whole episodes for whatever editorial reasons—or nonreasons—they might have. Thus the suggestion of one censor to substitute restaurant for the customary 18th-century tavern in a story about the American Revolution.

Restaurant is a French word not used in America for two generations after the Revolution. The same censor was told, apparently, to remove all the gods, damns, goddamns, etc. In one scene our narrator "began silently to pray, 'Oh, please God, oh please.'" The censor struck it. That same mindless censor also accepted our substitution of hard cider for wine, apparently wholly unaware that they both have the same alcoholic content. Hard cider is apple wine. The examples of this sort of mindlessness go on and on in uncounted tedium.

Lesson Number Three: Censors don't understand the context of the situation. Much that might appear on first glance to be merely simple mindlessness is often an inability to see the offending element in context. This might, for instance, explain a censor's failure to distinguish profanity from prayer. A common basis for censorship is to strike episodes that appear racist or sexist. Often these episodes are included in order to attack the very attitudes they display. The example of Daniel's racist remarks in *Jump Ship to Freedom* cited above is a good example. In *The Clock* we attack raw sexism in the workforce by focusing on a victim of it. We have been challenged for not having Annie stand up to her lecherous supervisor. But that was 1810—which leads me to ...

Lesson Number Four: Censors lack historical perspective—even of their own times. Books have been challenged for the use of the word Japs. But anyone who remembers the era of World War II at all knows that Jap was the universally employed term. Read some of the classic books written about that war. In John Hersey's *Into the Valley* about a battle on Guadalcanal in 1943, not only do the soldiers regularly use the term Jap but Hersey himself uses it in his narrative. Would a battle account of GI dialogue of 1943 ring true if the soldiers referred to their deadly enemies as Japanese? In my other life as a professional historian I work with Indians a good deal. They call themselves Indians. Must we have our frontiersmen in a novel about the expanding west say that the "only good Native American is a dead Native American." Yet I know of a young seventh-grade teacher who says she will not use a book that uses the term Indian. And how do we keep up with what are acceptable terms for Negroes, colored, blacks, African-Americans? Certainly we all agree not to use the word nigger when we can avoid it, but how real would it sound for Confederate troops in 1863 to say Negro—not to mention African-American. Would Huckleberry Finn be the same story if his companion was referred to as African-American Jim?

The lack of historical perspective, however, goes way beyond the use of historically acceptable terms. We have been informally challenged as sexist for having Willy in *War Comes to Willy Freeman* dress as a boy in order to be able to make her way from place to place through revolutionary era society. Apparently, many parents of young teenagers have so little understanding of the past that they fail to see how difficult—indeed nearly impossible—it would be for a fourteen-year-old black girl to travel alone through New York and Connecticut in 1782. On one occasion we had an editor change a statement made by a Revolutionary Era bandit from "You're acting like a couple of old women" to "You're acting like cowards." I think the dialogue loses a lot in that translation. How can youngsters of today ever understand the progress of women over the past generation if they don't know the situation of women in America in the past—indeed the traditional situation of women everywhere?

Lesson Number Five: The concerns of censors change over time. In the 1970s we were not made aware of objections—if there were any—to damns, goddamns, even son of a bitches. Objections to profanity (there is virtually no obscenity in our books) rose during the late 1970s and into the 80s. This fits the upward curve of the popularity of fundamentalist Protestantism. In the earlier era, the wake of the Vietnam peace movement, concerns centered on violence as depicted in our battle scenes. More recently, we have encountered objections to depictions of alcohol drinking—indeed, even the word tavern as I have already noted. And even more recently there have been the alleged violations of sex and racial sensitivities. Sometimes, if you just wait long enough, the censors will lose interest, though you can be sure that new ones—or the same old ones—will reappear with new concerns. They are always there.

Lesson Six: I have met the enemy and I am them.

Historians, of course, study change over time, and Lesson Six is one that time—not any censor—taught me. If an author is lucky enough to see his books still in print and selling briskly a generation after he wrote them, he must confront the very real possibility of a disjuncture between the audience he wrote the books for and the audience that is now reading them. The publishers of the Hardy Boys, Nancy Drew, and Tom Swift routinely update their old tales. It is especially true of the past thirty years that social change has been profound and rapid. The connotations expressed by certain words are not the same in 1998 as they were in 1974.

In 1939 Clark Gable's famous *Gone With the Wind* "damn!" was a shocker; to today's audiences it doesn't mean a thing. What I have seen over the past decade or so, however, is the reverse of the loss of shock value in certain words. Where damns, goddamns, hells, and Jesus Christ were strong shockers for fifth graders, but to their parents quite unexceptionable in 1974, this is no longer the case.

About ten or twelve years ago we began to hear from our middle-school readers complaints about the "swears" in our books. Why did we have to use them? I have already responded to that question. The one I want to deal with now, is what do you do when the social and intellectual climate change so much that words have a different effect on readers—indeed even mean something quite different to them?

Same words—different meaning. Similarly, in the verbal context of the early 1970s, the full and steamy wake of the free speech movement of the previous decade, it took a damn or a hell to carry any emotional weight. *The Bloody Country,* for example, is full of them, even on occasion in the mouths of nine-year-olds.

But the free speech waters rose to flood tide and beyond. The filth of speech on television and in films today has become so outrageous that a backwash was sure to come, and the tide ebbed with a rush. Parents are so disgusted with obscenities in the media that they are now much more aware and concerned about their kids' verbal encounters at school. Indeed, even some of the kids are concerned.

Thus a goddamn in 1998 carries a much heavier impact, believe it or not, than it did in 1974—or so, at least, our letters and conversations with young teenagers and their parents tell us. Indeed, that is the Lesson Six that I learned. I recently reread *The Bloody Country,* and found many of the curse words and especially the use of nigger, unnecessary, even grating on occasion. The lesson, of course, is that if the intellectual or cultural perspective of the readership changes, there can be actual changes in the received meaning of certain words. Thus what is not censorable in one era might certainly well be in another. The great question is, what should an author of a frequently reprinted book do about it? If the words on the page no longer get the intended response—one which they once did, should an author, given a chance, alter the words in his original? Should he, in other words, censor himself?

This gets me to the central authorial question. If you know certain elements of a situation are liable to offend some influential readers, why don't you just omit or change them? Let me tell you a story.

I earlier described the wrestling bout of Timmy and Betsy in *My Brother Sam Is Dead* over a note Timmy was carrying to Loyalist spies. In this scene Timmy fails in his effort to participate in the war and becomes thereafter an increasingly confused and distressed onlooker. In his political development it is a climactic moment. We had to give it some emotional impact. When the first draft came to me with Betsy's "You little bastard," (p. 84), I called my brother to tell him that the teenage daughter of the town's most respectable family would not have used that word. Not that folks in the olden days didn't—they used every word we do today, not excluding the f—- one. But Betsy wouldn't. "OK," says James, "what would she say?" "You little viper; you snake," I suggested. "Oh, come on; we're writing for teenagers in 1974. Those words carry no force at all." I had to agree; the literary needs outweighed the historical ones.

Over the years, I have asked hundreds of middle-school kids to suggest a phrase that their mothers would accept, but that would pack the same wallop. The best they have come up with so far goes like this:

Original Version

Then she jumped me. She caught me completely by surprise. She just leaped onto me and I fell down backwards and she was lying on top of me, trying to wrestle her hands down inside of my shirt. "Goddamn you, Betsy," I shouted. I grabbed her by her hair and tried to pull her head back, but she jerked it away from me. I began kicking around with my feet trying to catch her someplace where it would hurt, but she kept wriggling from side to side on top of me and I couldn't get in a good kick. I hit her on the back but in that position I couldn't get much force. "Get off me, Betsy."

"Not until I get that letter," she said. She jerked at my shirt, trying to pull it up. I grabbed at her hands and twisted my body underneath her to turn over so I would be on top, but she pushed her whole weight down on me, grunting. So I slammed her as hard as I could on the side of the head.

"You little bastard," she shouted. She let go of my shirt with one hand and slapped me as hard as she could across my face. My nose went numb and my eyes stung and tears began to come.

The Atlanta Journal
THE ATLANTA CONSTITUTION

PAGE 2-B, SATURDAY, JULY 16, 1983

Trying to kill reason itself

It is a tale of conflict, moral ambiguity and history.

A Tory father is pitted against his patriotic son during the American Revolution. Both believe they are right and both suffer. The story poses few easy questions and offers fewer easy answers. It is designed to make young minds consider in some depth the price of liberty.

Judging from the hullabaloo in Gwinnett County over the book, "My Brother Sam Is Dead," some older minds, as well, could use a refresher course on this subject. A group of parents wanted to ban the book from school library shelves, but, wisely, the school board said no. (The board did agree to place an edition abridged by the publisher in elementary schools.)

What's so objectionable? Well, it seems, "My Brother Sam Is Dead," contains a bit of salty language. Accordingly, some parents claim the book is "garbage" and predict it will lead to "moral decay."

The book is sprinkled with passages like this: " 'Damn it, that's rebellion,' one of the farmers said. 'They'll have us in war yet.' "

Or this: "He told Mr. Beach to go to hell and galloped his horse at Mr. Beach."

And at one point, we have this: " 'God, can't you do anything right, Tim?'

'Don't curse,' I said. 'It's a sin.' "

There are other bits of profanity, but it's hardly the stuff to scandalize young ears. In fact, it's talk that most students encounter daily on network television, in movies, on public sidewalks and, undoubtedly, on Gwinnett County school grounds.

In the book, such profanity adds dramatic emphasis and realism. It is not gratuitous. In any case, "My Brother Sam Is Dead" is not required reading in Gwinnett; it simply graces the system's supplemental reading lists.

Garbage? The American Library Association lauded the book as "a sobering tale that will leave readers with a more mature view of history and war." It was named a Newberry Honor Book and was nominated for a National Book Award in 1974, the year it was published.

In its narrative, the price of liberty is bloodshed, death and anguish within families. Its protagonist pays the ultimate price so that future generations may live in a republic of diverse views, cultures, religions and values.

Living in such a republic, of course, presents some challenges. In Gwinnett County, as elsewhere, our system demands a continuing sacrifice: We must tolerate diversity. We cannot define the world in our personal terms and force that definition on others. There are other points of view to consider, other values that must be allowed. We have the freedom to choose among them.

As John Milton observed three centuries ago: He who "kills a man kills a reasonable creature, God's image; but he who destroys a good book kills reason itself."

In 1885, The Committee of the Public Library of Concord, Mass., banned Mark Twain's "Huckleberry Finn" as "trash suitable only for the slums." Twain considered this "a rattling tiptop puff . . . (which) will sell 25,000 copies for us sure." Maybe the would-be censors of Gwinnett have ensured that "My Brother Sam Is Dead" will get an avid perusal by schoolchildren from Norcross to Buford. Maybe they have performed a public service.

Sanitized Version

Then she jumped me. She caught me completely by surprise. She just leaped onto me and I fell down backwards and she was lying on top of me, trying to wrestle her hands down inside of my shirt. "Curse you, Betsy," I shouted. I grabbed her by her hair and tried to pull her head back, but she jerked it away from me. I began kicking around with my feet trying to catch her someplace where it would hurt, but she kept wriggling from side to side on top of me and I couldn't get in a good kick. I hit her on the back but in that position I couldn't get much force. "Get off me, Betsy."

"Not until I get that letter," she said. She jerked at my shirt, trying to pull it up. I grabbed at her hands and twisted my body underneath her to turn over so I would be on top, but she pushed her whole weight down on me, grunting. So I slammed her as hard as I could on the side of the head.

"You bloody skunk," she shouted. She let go of my shirt with one hand and slapped me as hard as she could across my face. My nose went numb and my eyes stung and tears began to come.

A third version of the same episode was presented in an expurgated edition of the book that Scholastic put out (without consulting us) for its club distribution. It goes like this (pp. 96–97):

Then she jumped me. She caught me completely by surprise. She just leaped onto me and I fell down backwards and she was lying on top of me, trying to wrestle her hands down inside of my shirt. I grabbed her by her hair and tried to pull her head back, but she jerked it away from me. I began kicking around with my feet trying to catch her someplace where it would hurt, but she kept wriggling from side to side on top of me and I couldn't get in a good kick. I hit her on the back but in that position I couldn't get much force. "Get off me, Betsy."

"Not until I get that letter," she said. She jerked at my shirt, trying to pull it up. I grabbed at her hands and twisted my body underneath her to turn over so I would be on top, but she pushed her whole weight down on me, grunting. So I slammed her as hard as I could on the side of the head.

She let go of my shirt with one hand and slapped me as hard as she could across my face. My nose went numb and my eyes stung and tears began to come.

Perhaps opinion will differ as to which version makes the most memorable impression. My brother and I often disagree. But on this one, we do not.

When kids ask why we use all the "swears" in our books, I try to explain that you just can't have soldiers in battle saying "Goll ding it, I've been hit," or "I'm shot, good gracious." Readers know that is not what they said; the story would lose credibility and we would lose readers. Look again, for instance at the John Hersey's 1943 battle account I mentioned earlier. The much lesser public tolerance for profanity at mid century forced writers into pallid representations of dialogue.

Hersey's battle hardened GIs use phrases like "You can bet your shirt." One Marine captain, in rallying his scattering troops in the heat of deadly combat, says "Gosh, and they call you marines." Now we know he didn't say "gosh," and the use of the word in this context fails utterly to capture the spirit and emotion of the moment and casts an aura of unbelievability over the whole account.

Finally, let's confront the N word. *The Bloody Country*—on one level about interstate relations during the Confederation years—is on another level about the relative balance of property values and human values in the formative era of United States history. Ben Buck is the son of a mill owner—property values obviously symbolized by both the mill and the name Buck. His closest friend is the family slave, Joe Mountain. In the course of the story Ben realizes that if he loses the mill, he will end up a wage slave working for someone else and with little freedom of action or independent control over his life. Joe, on the other hand, learns that the only way he can gain his freedom is to get away from the mill. Ultimately he runs away.

We first encounter the N word on page 3. Joe was half Mohegan, and Ben says, "You're an Indian yourself." "Hell, I'm not an Indian," Joe Mountain says, "I'm a nigger." "Besides, if I'm not a nigger, how come I belong to your father? Indians can't be slaves, only niggers." (p. 4) This begins the development of our theme of the universal need for individual freedom. In the era of American slavery from the mid-17th century to 1865, whites— North and South—did not like to use the word slave. Note, for instance, that the U.S. Constitution written in 1787 condones the institution by referring to slaves as "persons . . . held to service or labor" and "persons imported." Nigger was a less embarrassing euphemism for slave. It was universally used that way. But let's try our dialogue again. Ben says "You're an Indian yourself." "Hell, I'm not an Indian," Joe Mountain says, "I'm a Negro." "Besides, if I'm not a Negro, how come I belong to your father? Indians can't be slaves, only Negroes." Try it again substituting African-American for Negro. Do you see what I mean?

Our use of the N word is intended to deepen the depiction of the misery of slavery and of the degraded status of free blacks as well. Most of our readers are white. It is our effort to convey to them the trials of people of African ancestry in North America. We want youngsters to understand the difficulties of growing up black in America. We think this is necessary for them to think knowledgeably and wisely about contemporary conditions about which they, as adult citizens, will have to make decisions affecting their own and others' lives. Without knowledge of the horrors and misery of the black—especially, slave—experience that has embarrassed America for centuries, future citizens cannot confront intelligently the racism that so degrades the nation. And without confronting it, they cannot rectify it.

This is our fundamental objective in the Arabus Trilogy. In *War Comes to Willy Freeman* we try to show the problems faced by the most powerless people—young, black, female, and slave. But in the end Willy struggles through, not happily, but free, at least. In *Jump Ship to Freedom,* Daniel learns firsthand the searing ambiguity of a Constitution for white freedom and black slavery. And in *Who Is Carrie?* our little black girl faces the awful future of never knowing if she is slave or free. In all of these novels the word nigger is unavoidable if anything close to historical verisimilitude is to be drawn. But beyond that, the word is necessary in order to portray the horrible condition of enslaved African-Americans in a way that evokes an emotional response that draws the reader into the story.

We know that our approach to the historical roots of the nation's race problem works. These books are used in largely black-populated inner city schools. We get approving fan letters from students there. One eighth grader wrote from New Jersey, "This week I picked up the book *Jump Ship to Freedom* and I could not put it down. I am a black girl who of course has heard many things about the black situation but I've never really got into it. When I read this book, a whole new world opened up to me. My mother is buying the other two volumes today.

"Thank you for writing these books. Sometimes children my age with all the things I have and my beautiful home need to experience other things." Indeed, an eighth-grade teacher wrote from Austin, Texas, after having read *Willy* and *Jump Ship* asking for a photo: "I really do think that many of my students will be surprised to discover that you are of African-American descent." After seeing my picture, she wrote, "I still plan to use your books during Black History month. . . ."

It should be clear by now that as we write we use neither curse words nor racial slurs without giving them thorough consideration. We do not use nigger when some other term will do as well. Nor do we say goddamn when we could say gosh with just as great an effect. As a matter of fact, the number of complaints we received from middle schoolers about "swears" in our books caused us to write our last two books with almost none. It was not easy. A partial solution was to make the two fourteen- or fif-

December 7, 1996

The Star
Chicago Heights, IL.

To the Editors:

We have recently become aware of the controversy in your area over our book, "War Comes to Willy Freeman." While we regret that it caused some discomfort to one student, we still believe that the book ought to be used in your schools.

"War Comes to Willy Freeman" is part of a trilogy about a black family during the American Revolution. It was designed specifically to heighten awareness among school children to the suffering endured by blacks under slavery. The book has won many awards, and has been read by millions of children in thousands of American schools. It is routinely assigned in inner city schools, where students, teachers, and administrators are largely black.

We did not introduce the offending word lightly, but only after long discussions between ourselves and with our editor. We ultimately concluded that no other word would present black history truthfully. That we do not condone casual use of the word is made clear in the epilogue to the book. While it is true that in rare instances there have been objections to the word "nigger" in the dialogue, by far the majority of black parents and educators believe that their students ought to be given a realistic view of the horrors of slavery. We will do nothing to ameliorate conditions for blacks if we pretend that those conditions do not exist. Surely nobody would want us to present slave owners as speaking courteously to their slaves.

In assigning "War Comes to Willy Freeman," Ms. Comandella was only doing what thousands of other American teachers with black students in their classrooms have been doing for fifteen years. We hope that concerned parents will take the time to read "War Comes to Willy Freeman" to see if they really think, it is "racially insensitive."

Cordially,

James Lincoln Collier

LETTER PUBLISHED IN *THE STAR*, DECEMBER 15, 1996

teen-year-old protagonists in *With Every Drop of Blood* old-fashioned fundamental Christians, given to quoting the Bible rather than spouting profanity. In that book we got rid of much of the profanity that would have been standard among soldiers, and we tried to use the N word only when absolutely necessary. In this scene fourteen-year-old Johnny has just been captured by a black Union soldier, Cush, and wrestles with his world turned upside down. "Taking orders from a darky was another shock, especially one my own age. It was just the strangest thing, for I'd never heard a darky even speak back to a white person, much less give them orders." This works, but wouldn't the sense of shock and role reversal be a lot more intense if the N word was used instead of darky? And, in any event, are 20th-century African-Americans any less offended by darky than nigger?

The American Library Association Office for Intellectual Freedom has all sorts of guides and other materials to help deal with efforts at school and library censorship—more especially how to head it off at the pass before it erupts into a major community battle. But I have a few suggestions that might help avoid even the thought of challenging the books you choose to use in class. Make sure your books are grade-level appropriate. Consider carefully whether you should read them to students, have students read out loud in class, silently in class, or at home. Communities differ radically in their tolerance for obscenity, profanity, and racial and gender slurs. Be sensitive to those levels of tolerance. But in the end, the choice of classroom materials belongs to the professional, not the parents. Parents may know what is best for their own children, but teachers are better judges of what's best for the whole class.

BIOGRAPHIES

James Lincoln Collier

James Lincoln Collier was born in New York City in 1928. He grew up in Garden City, New York and Wilton, Connecticut, where he attended local schools. He graduated from Hamilton College in 1950. After serving stateside in the U.S. Army during the Korean War, he worked as a magazine editor in New York for six years, writing part-time, primarily fiction. In 1958 he became a full-time writer, contributing to many national magazines, and beginning his career in books. He published his first children's books in 1965, and subsequently has written more than thirty-five works for young people on a variety of subjects, both fiction and nonfiction. Nine of these have been collaborations with Christopher.

In 1978 he published his jazz history, *The Making of Jazz*, which proved to be a landmark in the field. He has written more books on jazz, as well as a number of scholarly articles in the field. Additionally, he has published in the area of social history and the social sciences generally. He has been a Fellow of the National Endowment for the Humanities, and a Research Fellow of the Institute for Studies in American Music. His books have won numerous prizes, including the Newbery Honors Medal, the Child Study Association's Best Book Award, the Jane Addams Peace Prize, the Chritopher Award, and others. He has twice been a finalist for the National Book Award. He is an avocational jazz musician, and plays regularly in jazz bands in New York City.

Christopher Collier

Christopher Collier was born in New York City in 1930. Since 1938 he has lived in Connecticut where he completed public school in Wilton and Westport. He earned a B.A. at Clark University in Worcester, Mass., and an M.A. and Ph.D. in History from Columbia University. He served as a bandsman in Texas during the Korean War in 1952 and 1953.

All his life since then has been spent teaching history, first in junior and senior high school and, since 1961, at the college level. He is the author of several books and numerous scholarly and popular articles about the history of Connecticut. Since 1984 he has been Professor of History at the University of Connecticut and the official Connecticut State Historian. Christopher is the father of two sons and a daughter, and lives with his wife, Bonnie, a librarian, in Orange, Connecticut. He plays trumpet in a dance band and engages in several sports, principally figure skating.

In addition to the eight novels discussed in this handbook, the Colliers have published *Decision in Philadelphia: The Convention of 1787* (Random House/Ballantine, 1985, 1986), an adult, non-fiction work about the writing of the U.S. Constitution, and "The Drama of American History," a fifteen-volume narrative and descriptive history of the United States published by Marshall Cavendish of Tarrytown, N.Y. (1998-99).

At least two articles based on interviews with the Collier brothers have been published.

Hughes Moir. "Profile: James and Christopher Collier, More than Just a Good Read." *Language Arts.* 55 (March, 1978) 3.

Allen Raymond. "Jamie and Kit Collier: The Writer and the Historian." *Teaching Pre K-8.* January 1988.

They were also biographed in the series, "Meet the Newbery Authors," a video-cassette available from McGraw-Hill.

James Lincoln Collier and Christopher Collier are included in the standard biographical directories of authors of works for children as well as *Contemporary Authors.*

NEW YORK

NEW YORK

HUDSON RIVER

BEN'S ROUTE

COBB

WILKES BARRE

SUSQUEHANNA RIVER

VERPLANKS

DA

PENNSYLVANIA

NEW YORK CITY

NEWARK

WILLY'S

L

TRENTON

DAN'S ROUTE

PHILADELPHIA

DELAWARE RIVER

NEW JERSEY

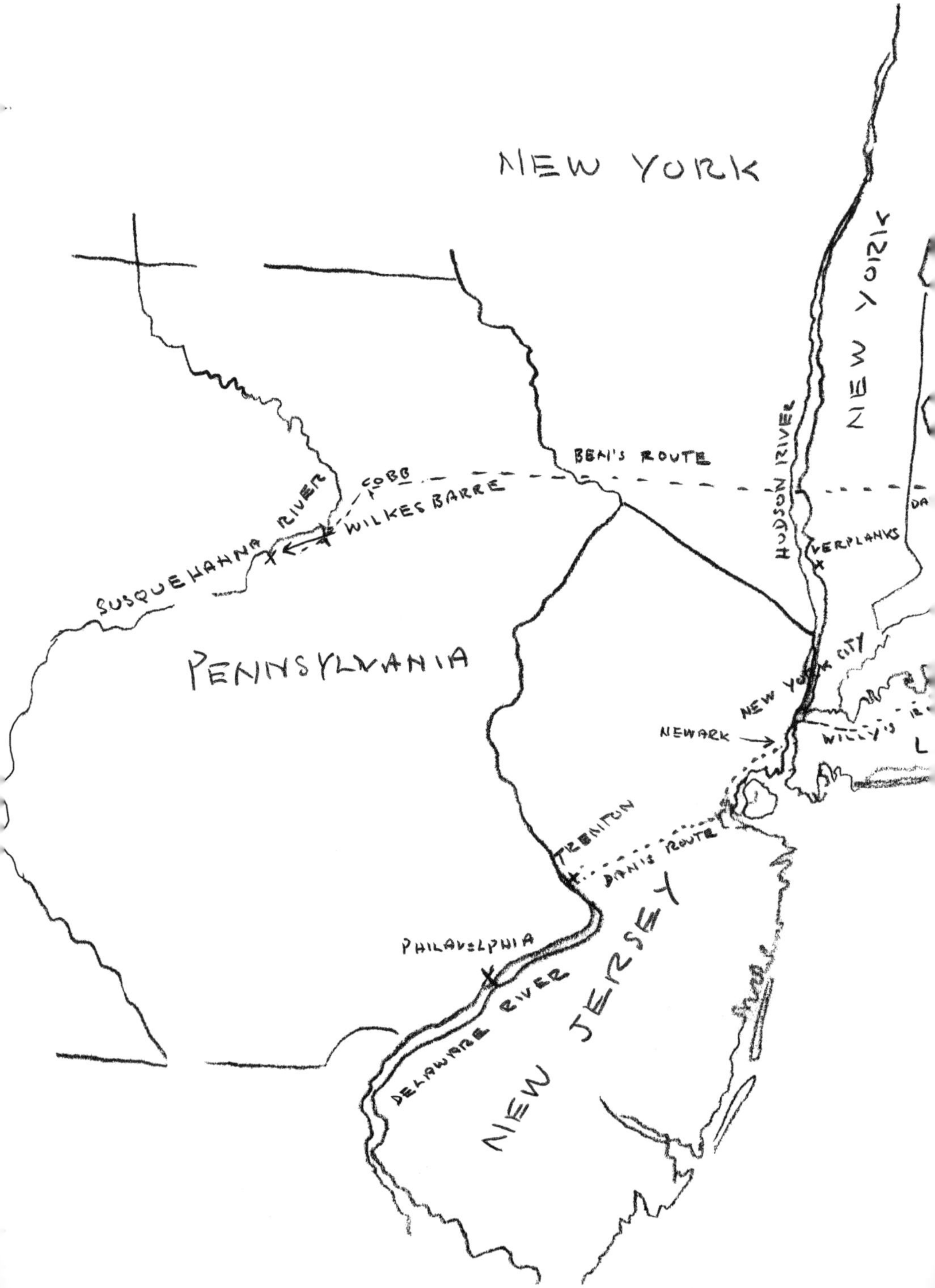